Dynamic Identities in Cultural and Public Contexts

D1557854

Dynamic Identities in Cultural and Public Contexts

Ulrike Felsing, Design2context, ZHdK

Lars Müller Publishers

I.
On Signifying, Showing, and Naming

An investigation of a specific type of appearance [Erscheinungs-weise] of visual identities [Erscheinungsbildern] with which specific institutions, in turn, make an appearance [Erscheinung] is confronted with several phenomena and questions that touch on more than the interests of designers and of corporate design. This applies both to the concept of visual identities in general as it does to the actual subject of this investigation, "dynamic" visual identities.

With the German term 'Erscheinungsbild' [literally "appear-ance picture"–Trans.], the visual representations of organiza-tions make use of a central philosophical reflection: that appearances are understood as a perceptible presence and rep-resentation of another reality — as is the case for Plato with appearances and ideas, and for Kant with appearances and the "Ding an sich" (thing-in-itself). The simplest type of relationship is based upon the common idea that in the design of a visual identity the manifoldness of a thing is envisioned which is not easily brought into view, as is precisely the case with institu-tions and organizations.

In this way, the perceptive and notional operations of concepts of reality can now be understood as a whole. All our figurative, conceptual, linguistic, logical, causal, narrative, and other visu-alizations of reality are operations insofar as they bring what is manifold into a certain connection and visualize it as a unity. Kant very fundamentally called everything that relates to our perceptions and conceptions 'one' common representation, that "I" always connect all my conceptions and perceptions together when "I" in each case actually think of them as 'mine': "'I think,' must necessarily be capable of accompanying all our represen-tations." [01] This would then be the overall, fundamental con-

[01] Immanuel Kant, Critique of Pure Reason [1781], trans. J. M. D. Meiklejohn (London, 1855), p. 82.

ception of unity that all other connecting activities of logic, of causality, of representation, etc. have as a prerequisite. The "visual identities" dealt with here are but 'one' albeit elaborated type of these conceptions.

However, at the same time it makes a significant difference whether we view these operations with regard to 'recognition' or 'identification.' Conventional philosophical investigations refer to the cognitive process, which raises the question of what the various operations mentioned to bring the manifold into a certain whole 'make recognizable' about appearances. However, the pronounced sense of "visual identities" takes the same operations as a rhetorical compendium with which something manifold is 'to be identified' in a visual identity in one or another expedient way.

The difference between recognizing and identifying shines some light into the twilight zone of the term "Identität" in the German version of the professional design term "identity," which Ulrike Felsing herself consistently avoids in the German title and text of this study. "Identität" can mean both 'making something recognizable' as something, as well as 'making something identifiable' as something. Whereas the professional English term "identity," for example in the expression "corporate identity," undoubtedly has the meaning of identifying, its transation into German at once makes it dubious.

Let us return to appearances and their manifoldness, visual identities and their conceptions of connection and unity. The questions about both recognition and identification strike in a different direction when they are posed for the relationship of various appearances on the one hand and various visual identities on the other. To what extent can variable appearances, once again, allow a connecting factor to be recognizable among the manifold, and to what extent can variable visual identities, once again, make a connecting factor identifiable among the manifold? For the first case there is the change in form, for which a butterfly's metamorphosis over time is a notable example, in that the various chronologically successive forms of appearance, of egg, caterpillar, chrysalis, and imago, are understood to belong to 'one' type of insect called a butterfly.

This investigation by Ulrike Felsing takes up the analogous case of one feature of visual identities which she calls "dynamic": the representation of certain institutions such as museums and exhibition and event venues which use visual metamorphoses in their visual identities (e.g. to the rhythm of their changing events). In the process, this mutability, the "dynamic" itself, becomes part of what is to be identified about the institution. The Catholic Church has also made use of this in the repeating liturgical color changes over the course of the ecclesiastical year (e.g. white, red, purple, green, black).

The subject of this investigation is various processes for the creation of such mutability and dynamics — which, however, at the same time follow the requirement of identifying what remains continuously and coherently present in the dynamic variety of these visual identities — the construction of change as identification of distinctiveness. However, in contrast to the artistic aspect of this process and the rules of image and form transformation employed, the intent does not vary in order to expediently connect to and make identifiable a manifold something.

Of course — to take hair-splitting to extremes — one can again
look at both the process as well as what should be made identifiable with it so that they make something completely different
recognizable. This sounds more complicated than it is, and in
common jargon is otherwise called ideological criticism. The subject of investigation of ideological criticism is to a certain extent
nothing other than the difference between an asserted reality
and what this assertion interestingly conceals about reality.

In the context understood here of identity as 'making identifiable,'
the historian Valentin Groebner from Lucerne coined the aptly
polemical expression, "We believe in the belief of others." [02]
The difference between such ideology production via marketing
and the shaping power of critical design practice would possibly be identifiable as this: by the transparency of 'making identifiable' serves the other perspective of what is recognizable — by
an identification which does not call for "belief" but recognition, cognizance, and thus "credibility."

Ulrike Felsing expressly devotes her investigations of dynamic
visual identities to the use of contemplative artistic processes
and rule constructions with which can follow "dynamic" visual
identities. However, in the process she subtly enough drew the
examples to be examined largely from a field of investigation that
still remains more accessible with respect to this critical distinction: cultural organizations, such as the Cinémathèque française,
which use some of the processes of "dynamic visual identities"
investigated here and apply what is identified to recognition, cognizance, and credibility.

The scriptures of the Old Testament took the final logical step
with regard to mistrust of 'making identifiable': "I am who I am"

and "Thou shalt not make unto thee ... any likeness." There is no avoiding the Old Testament god figure, neither in connotation nor in the imagination, not even by a name. The figure without qualities, without face and shape, and without name. What was it about the signifying, the showing, and the naming that was so ungodly or godless? With the concepts of signifying, showing, and naming it is certainly the hubris of being able to or only wanting to 'make something identifiable,' instead of 'making something recognizable,' the hubris of putting something else in place of the ostensibly signified, shown, and named. This Old Testament loquacity about the ineffable is for its part a significant, shaping rhetoric of unconditional "belief." In order to forestall any reification it effectively risks absolutely no mistake in the use of signifying, showing, or naming. It is an elocution, a literary form and appearance, and an endorsement of visual identities; a model for all "negative dialectics" and all "critique of instrumental reason."

To risk this mistake — unlike the Old Testament — for the sake of the credibility which should expect no "belief" from "the others" — unlike marketing — but rather a critical, engaged understanding: these would be visual identities which also always bring to fulfillment something of the shaping power of social vitality.

[02] Valentin Groebner, Identität – oder was die Anderen sich so vorstellen (Identity – or what the others imagine by it). Lecture at the MAZ Jubiläum (Swiss college of journalism), March 13, 2009, www.unilu.ch/files/
MAZ-Vortrag-360_Groebner_Vortrag.pdf (accessed 6/10/09), p. 5: "Because it (the key concept of identity)
stands for other people's illusions: for something that we do not believe ourselves but we are convinced that
the others are convinced of it — but not necessarily our colleague at the next desk, rather the other others,
the general public as they are also called, those out there everywhere. In a book worth reading, 'Wir glauben
an den Glauben der Anderen' (We believe in the belief of others), the Austrian cultural theorist Robert Pfaller
called this 'illusions without owners'." This expression aptly describes what I mean by 'making identifiable'
as opposed to 'making recognizable': an effect in which the instrumental subject is concealed.

II.
About the Investigation

The subjects of this investigation are flexible visual identities and the specific variation processes with which they are developed. Superordinate criteria characterizing flexible visual identities are offered while critical appraisal remains in the background. The investigation moves between three reference levels. In the main level, using case studies and examples, different processes will be presented with which flexible visual identities can be developed. One of the aims over the course of this investigation is to describe general principles of variation processes that may serve as inspiration for future design processes. Rather than strict formulas, these investigations provide examples that can be translated or adapted to other design problems, or to other fields. Flexible visual identities are characterized by variability, context-relatedness, processuality, performativity, non-linearity, coherency, and variety — and are found in varying degrees in the visual identities. The prevailing variation process employed determines how the visual identity is characterized. These characteristics — in a broader sense, aspects of flexibility and dynamics — are not only discussed as they relate to flexible visual identities, but also to distinct artistic projects and formative processes in nature, which appear in brief annotations parallel to the main text level. Reading the two levels in conjunction with each another generates a reciprocal understanding of the common process for the design of flexibility and dynamics. "Variegate, create references, transfer"— this investigation not only aims to describe something, but also literally demonstrates it. The manner of writing — in a sense, an essayistic approach that forms constellations — and the kind of design — the two parallel levels in the book — create the conditions which, upon reading, can continually provide new perspectives on "flexibility and dynamics." The different perspectives are interlaced and open up new questions, and thus create a third level of reference: an open process

of reading, interpretation, questioning, and understanding.
The majority of the case studies selected for this investigation
exhibit at least one of the criteria for a fully developed visual
identity. And one of the main criteria is fulfilled when the variations go beyond the mere playing with form to reflect an aspect
of a real, contentual characteristic. The interaction between
an organization, its contents, and their visualization defines the
quality of the visual identity. Rather than ideal or symbolic values,
the actual context should define these contents. A broad spectrum
of means is used for the visual representation of fully developed
visual identities, including staged projections, interfaces, and
networked presentations. However, they only produce an impression — presence, eventfulness, and surprise — when they are
grounded in terms of content and concept.
"Whereas Otl Aicher's effort towards a convincing visual identity
aimed for an argumentative connection on the basis of rational
penetration and ordered representation, communication in virtual,
electronic space rather softens the previously clear contours, as
far as the replacement of content explanations through the form
of presentation. The value of emotional experience and functional
use convince more directly and immediately than communicating through argument." [01] With the typogram developed by Otl
Aicher for the company ERCO, the characteristic behavior of light
makes the signet significant and gives it substance. The quality
of experience that is created through electronic media needs this
contentual substance, without which the media would degen-
erate into an arbitrary white noise. However, for fully developed
visual identities it is not only a question of implementing the
change of media between light and typography (as with ERCO),
but rather of continuing it with other media. Furthermore, it is
crucial to use media in accordance with its particular characteristics rather than as a fashionable effect.

[01] Walter Bauer-Wabnegg, Die Marke als Medium: Vom digitalen zum virtuellen Unternehmen,
          in: Kompendium Corporate Identity und Corporate Design, p. 84.

Another criterion for fully developed visual identities is a broad spectrum of variation: a design principle or basic theme permits its implementation in various forms of expression, dimensions, or media — in contrast to the variation of a single element. The broad range of choices made available by computers makes it possible for the designer to work with a far greater number of signs. But the question is: Is he then still designing?

Another criterion, which is at the same time one of the main functions of flexible visual identities, is differentiation. It creates the tension in dynamic visual identities. A distinction can then be made, for example, between the association as a whole and its subsections, between permanent presence and temporary events, and between various communication media.

Broad research into currently available examples as well as the case studies taken up in this publication indicate that it is mainly organizations [02] in the cultural and public sectors that are represented by flexible visual identities. What are the possible reasons for this tendency? Are the views of clients and designers more tradition-bound and simple in the corporate world? And in contrast, more open in the cultural sector? Is it perhaps even a kind of status symbol in the cultural sector to represent oneself with a flexible, processual visual identity? These questions are examined in chapter IV in relation to the impact of flexible visual identities.

[02] "Organization" is used in this investigation to mean public, social, cultural, and educational institutions.

III.
What Are Flexible Visual Identities?

Flexibility

"'Flexibility' first appeared in the English vocabulary in the fifteenth century, and at first signified a specific relationship of pliancy and inertia in the plant world: 'Its meaning originally derived from the simple observation that though a tree may bend in the wind, its branches spring back to their original position.' Since then the word has experienced a shift in meaning which redresses the original tension: today stability is always regarded as torpidity. Flexibility now means the same as the capacity of continually and quickly adapting to change; it is no longer oriented towards a return to an original state but is always directed towards the future." [03]

"The German-language version of Wikipedia defines flexibility as 'basically the dissolution of formerly rigid structures…. In business, flexibility describes the transition from the comprehensive contractually regulated employment conditions of Fordism (normal employment contract, fixed working hours, fixed wages according to collective agreements, sick pay and holiday pay, protection against unfair dismissal) to the organi-

Flexibility is a concept that we principally associate with the idea of physical or mental maneuverability. In a figurative sense we need it, among other things, for the human ability to adapt to changing situations. Flexibility can be a central feature of a visual identity when the basic concept is refashioned in such a way that not only the constant but also the variable factors can come into play.

With what do these factors combine? Constancy and variability can be produced either within a sign through its various aspects (characteristics), or through various elements of the visual identity as a whole. Two different sides combine in a sign: that of the expression of the sign (the signifier) and that of the content of the sign (the signified). The signifier has various aspects, including form, color, brightness, size, proportion, perspective, and degree of abstraction. The signifier is additionally characterized by the tool used for its representation — e.g., drawing pen, pencil, or computer drawing — or the specific display medium — poster, webpage, or video projection.

In principle, constant and variable aspects can be distinguished. In a flexible visual identity, constancy and variability can be produced through each individual sign because both constant and variable aspects coincide within the sign. One example is the visual identity for 2000 en France, in which the container — the circular area with the lines of text which move around it in the shape of a vortex — is a constant aspect, and its content — the inner area—a variable aspect. In the process of animation, the "Gestalt," the essence of the sign, is mostly preserved and the form is changed, as the EXPO 2000 case study illustrates.

However, constancy and variability can also be produced through different elements of the visual identity as a whole. Such as with the visual identity of the Museum Boijmans van Beuningen Rotterdam, where "Boijman's font" is a fixed component while

[03] Thomas Lemke, Flexibilität, in: Glossar der Gegenwart, p. 82; Lemke cites from Richard Sennett's book The Corrosion of Character: The Personal Consequences of Work in the New Capitalism.

the other typographical elements are variable and thus create a specific reference to the temporary exhibitions. Constancy may also be created through a fixed element, such as the typographic logo in the visual identity of the Frankfurter Kunstverein. Such an element has a similar effect to a logo in visual identities without variable components. In this investigation, these are called "static visual identities." In other cases, such a logo-like sign is simultaneously the most reduced form of the visual identity. In it, the constant shows itself in its purest form, as illustrated for example by the visual identity of the Cinémathèque française. This sign is called the "basic logo" in this investigation. To make a distinction, the logo of a static visual identity is called a "singular logo."

In the visual identities of the Kigali Convention Center, Rwanda, and Museion – Museum für moderne und zeitgenössische Kunst, Bozen, a constant design principle runs like a thread through the various forms of expression and dimensions. This means that in each sign there is something that all of them have in common: the design principle. However, the form of expression changes with every implementation. It is similar when a basic theme is translated into various media and formats. The Cinémathèque française and Quartier des spectacles case studies show that the "elemental" can produce constancy between very heterogeneous media, as between the graphic simulation of "light" and the real projection of "light." Constancy is also created through stylistic means, which correspond with the personal style of the designer and standard and convention. Additional constancy is produced as a result of regularity, for example basing a design on a constant grid — as shown by the visual identity of "Ffm Lounge." Constancy increases if the design constant is supported by a wide range of content-related reference levels. All these factors counteract a possible dissolution, i.e. splintering into

zation of employment to a large degree without fixed specifications…. In society flexibility refers to the fundamental changes in social insurance systems (here partly almost meaning the same as privatization).'… The most influential scientific contribution to the flexibility debate in recent years was certainly formulated by the American sociologist Richard Sennett (1998). He assigns several characteristic features to the concept of flexibility. Breaking out of blind routine, de-bureaucratization, openness to short-term change, and less dependency upon rules and formal procedures are pitted against permanent risk and the loss of security as negative aspects." [04]

The term "flexible" is used in this investigation in the sense of adaptable: fully developed flexible visual identities can adapt to specific content, situations, and contexts. They have the ability to react to changes in the organization and/or its context. "Flexibility" is closely connected with "variation" and "processuality." Flexible visual identities are based on the interplay of constant and variable signs. The "processual" is what is

    [04] www.flexibleatart.ufg.ac.at/main.php?id=abschluss&zufall=5.

being created or is passing, the open form, the provisional, the transition. But "processual" can also mean "being performed"; the signs take on something gestural-performative, they create presence, are eventful, and emphasize the atmospheric and transitory. This investigation explores the significant features of "processual visual identities" and not the process of their design development in the sense of "corporate design is a process." [05] "Dynamic visual identity" is used here as a superordinate term. Rather than the term "corporate design," which carries the connotation of a corporate and business culture, the term "visual identity" is used. It is closer to the field of design, of making and becoming visible, of presenting and communicating.

disjointed elements. Because the instruments of a flexible visual identity are neither uniform nor constantly repeated, constancy can only be achieved via other factors. The focus of the case studies examined in chapters 1–6 is therefore on both constant as well as variable factors.

What is the effect produced by the different processes with which both constancy and variability are created? In what contexts are they appropriate, and in which less so? These questions are examined in detail in chapter IV.

What are the functions of the constant and variable aspects? The constant aspects ensure that a visual identity is recognizable despite variation. In many of the visual identities investigated here, the constant aspects convey fundamental contents and the variable aspects the changing contents of an organization. Basic information can be tied to constant contents — the general as opposed to the particular, permanent as opposed to temporary events. In some visual identities the constant elements represent the entire corporation and the variable elements their subsections. Other visual identities convey what is superordinate with constant elements and what is individual with variable elements. For example, in the visual identity for the millennium celebrations in France, 2000 en France, the silhouette, like a mask, is the constant element of the sign. It symbolizes the globe, our "world community," that is encircled by a kind of layer of immaterial information. During the course of the development of the visual identity, various designers fill the circular area with different images and text, which represent their personal ideas about the future — of the year 2000.

In the visual identity of the Museum Boijmans van Beuningen Rotterdam, the constant elements represent the "static parts" of the museum, and the variable elements the temporary exhibitions. "Within the museum, Mevis & Van Deursen's Boijman's

font is used to indicate what the designers describe as the 'static
features' (the lifts, the restaurant, the shop).... In tandem with
the custom font, Mevis & Van Deursen employ a different typeface
for the signage and print associated with each of the Boijmans'
temporary exhibitions. In choosing these faces, they bear in mind
both the subject matter of the show and how the type relates to
the others on display." [06] The interplay of constant and variable
elements is the basis of flexibility. It is crucial for a fully developed
flexible visual identity that, respectively, variable aspects refer
to specific content and constant aspects to the constant, most
fundamental, content. With fully developed flexible visual identities this referencing is established from the beginning through
the basic theme or the design principle.
How do the constant and variable elements come into being in a
visual identity? The constant and variable elements are derived
from an extensive analysis of the organization, its context, and
its essential characteristics, and are grounded in a basic theme,
a design principle, or on open rules. But what does "open" mean
here? An example: for the visual identity of the Galerie für zeitgenössische Kunst, Leipzig, [07] it was determined that only the
location and date was to be specifically emphasized as a main
recognition feature. "Here and now. This is how the work of the
gallery could be characterized ... The activities take place in
Leipzig and also for Leipzig.... It underlines that the regional reference is important for Leipzig." [08] However, the signifier of
these two content constants is variable: for example, it can vary
in typography and color. It is therefore possible to respond to
the specific implementation with the instruments of the visual
identity. While rules are used in static visual identities to stipu-
late the design of elements such as logo, typeface, format, or
design pattern, with the visual identity of the Galerie für zeitgenössische Kunst, the rule is formulated in a more general sense,

[06] Angus Hyland, c/id: Visual Identity and Branding for the Arts, p. 113. [07] The visual identity was used
          during the period from autumn 1996 until spring 2000. [08] Das Gesicht des Museums, Bogen 4a.

The "overall design becomes a 'signet'"

The agency co-founded by Karl Gerstner, Gerstner, Grediger + Kutter (GGK), began developing integrated advertising campaigns in the sixties: "You have to think back to a time when the idea had not been contemplated that you must also in fact translate complex tasks in a complex way. I remember that before World War I advertising mainly consisted of making a poster or an advertisement. Talk of campaigns came relatively late. That was a task requiring a concept in order to form a network." [10] According to Gerstner, this networking should couple the individual tasks together so that a "continuous line is created." [11] For this purpose, content and a connective aesthetic principle were adapted for the various media: "Communication on a poster takes place under different conditions than an advertisement, which can be viewed at relatively close proximity and leisure." [12] As today this approach seems self-evident, it is all the more surprising that while content— message — is often adapted to the given communication media, visual

i. e. only the content constant is specified. The openness of the rule, the basic theme, or the design principle enables implementation in various forms of expression, dimensions, formats, and media.

The variable aspects are a result of variation, and thus the particular variation process is fundamental for the visual identity. The variations develop by transferring "something": into another form, color, or materiality; into another form of representation; or into another medium. With fully developed flexible visual identities, the variations appear not only successively, but also in parallel, e. g. within signage in an interior, on communication media, and outside a building. Other constant and/or variable aspects are derived from visual elements, as described in the next section in relation to the "given references."

Rather than mere design methods that create variance, variation processes are important in determining the type of result, namely whether the flexible visual identity is based on a logo variation or on a sign family; or whether it is a "visual language"— a language-like visual identity. In this investigation, a logo-like sign that appears in several variants is called a "logo variation." A sign family is a group made up of various visual signs that relate to a common basic theme or design principle. In language-like visual identities, nearly every aspect of this writing-based communication incorporates the constant of the visual identity. Here the pretension expressed by Karl Gerstner in conversation is realized: "One day I noticed that it doesn't make sense, you make a signet and always add it somewhere. The design itself must take the place of the signet." [09] Visual identities in which the overall design takes over the function of the signet are fully developed integrated visual identities that can adapt to specific situational contexts. However —"Vital question: can a mark be variable without at the same time forfeiting its mark-like character? Counter-

[09] Karl Gerstner, personal interview, 2007.   [10] Ibid.   [11] Ibid.   [12] Ibid.

question: what is typical about a mark, the proportion or the 'configuration'? My answer is known: it is not and cannot be a question merely of proportions as such. Proportions can never be anything but good (or bad) relative to the task…. The ˋconfiguration̍ must not suffer as a result of the variability." [13]

One of the central questions posed by the development of flexible visual identities is encapsulated in the Italian translation of "Corporate Design": "Immagine coordinata"— it is a matter of the coordination of signs and the creation of connection (coherency). How can various images and signs be connected with each other so that a coherent family becomes recognizable? How can coherency be continuously created with dynamic, previously unspecified parameters? On one side the constant aspects ensure that the connection between the variations is recognizable; they create coherency or counterbalance the dissolution. However, above all, the connection between the variations is created via "given references" or "constructed, synthesized references." "Given references" are based upon the laws of geometry or color theory: "There is no dimension, proportion, form; no colour, which cannot be constantly led over into another. All the elements occur in series, or better, in groups." [14] "Given references" among colors and forms are used, for example, in the visual identity of the ABM Warenhauskette and that of SSH Utrecht, which is based upon a passport-like portrait composed of four saturated colors corresponding to background, hair, face, and clothes. The colors green, orange, red, yellow, brown, beige, blue, and violet are each applied in one light and one dark variation. Despite the changing forms — the hairstyles and clothes of the portraits vary — the "given references" create coherency among the colors and thus also consistency.

identities and / or logos are generally not. They continue to be applied as rigid appendages to all media — no matter whether they appear in print, on the Internet, or are representational or atmospheric.

What is "Gestalt" (form)?

The terms "form" and "Gestalt" (form) touch on one another in their meaning, but "Gestalt" can nevertheless not be explained by "form." "Gestalt" describes the essential, the elemental. "Gestalt" means "that something can emerge from given sensuous elements being beside or after each other that cannot be expressed by them or measured…. With an older description it can also be said it is a whole, but it must be added that they are not a summative whole but in the moment in which they are created they bring a special quality into the world which is different from their elements." [15] "For the Gestalt theoretician, the prime example of such a not merely additive but structuring or 'designed' whole was the melody…. When it is heard there is not something new there besides the notes, intervals, and times,

     [13] Karl Gerstner, Designing Programmes, p. 70. [14] Ibid., p. 17. [15] Robert Musil, cited in: Martin Menges, Abstrakte Welt und Eigenschaftslosigkeit, p. 97.

but rather with them. The melody does not come as a supplement but as a second way of appearing, a special form of existence." [17]

Continuous discontinuous

"Given references" are based on laws of geometry; or more precisely, they are based on the fact that visual elements are continuous.

"Colours are of their nature continuous. A series from white to black, e. g. in ten steps, each step the same size as the next and the one preceding it. Here the question is not one of counting but one of measuring. What is measured is the distance between two points. Between white and black there may be ten steps, or two, or two hundred (the human eye cannot distinguish more): a certain grey will always occupy the same place, an exactly intermediate shade of grey will occupy a place exactly in the centre between black and white, and so forth. But not only white will pass over continuously into black but any colour into any other colour. Colours form a closed system. But not only colours but all the elements of the

From a certain "difference" among the elements, it can no longer be said that they "naturally" refer to each other. Such references are "constructed references" of the designer, the direct expression of the design principle incorporated into the visual identity, used for example in the visual identity of Flughafen Köln-Bonn. They are not only references between single signs, but rather more between their diverse levels, especially when it is a question of complex signs, images, and language. By revealing such unfamiliar connections, the designer makes it possible for viewers to rediscover them. They can be of a narrative nature; they can produce humor, dislocation, and surprise.

Flexible visual identities often present intermediate stages within a certain variation spectrum. For example, the Twin Cities visual identity uses not only a Grotesk and an Antiqua typeface, but also their intermediate forms. [16] With a large number of intermediate stages, morphing-like transitions are created, and when animated a fluid movement.

The principle steps in the development of a flexible visual identity will now be described using the example of the visual identity of the Kigali Convention Center, Rwanda. This case study is particularly appropriate for this purpose because the design principle was visually derived in a systematic manner, and the derivation process documented. Essentially three different phases can be determined: (a) the analysis of the organization, (b) the development of constants and variables, and (c) the concrete implementation in which the situational-based variations are created. The organization and the designer collaborate as closely as possible on the analysis, which provides the necessary content aspects without which it is only possible to fall back upon conventions or common symbols. In the analysis, the organization

[16] Example of the metamorphosis, www.letterror.com/portfolio/twin/RN_AW_IR_NP.mov.
[17] Martin Menges, Abstrakte Welt und Eigenschaftslosigkeit, p. 97.

and its local context are examined, which serves primarily to identify features that characterize the organization. Rather than ideal or symbolic values, the actual context determines the questions: what distinguishes the organization from other similar organizations? What is special about its place and time, its cultural, historical, or geographical context, its architecture, its program? Are the architectural features particularly significant and do they shape, in a general sense, the urban or rural context? What distinguishes the core, the general level of the organization, and what are the exceptions?

The Kigali Convention Center is situated in an agriculture-intensive region of East Africa. The cultivated areas of the family farms are densely nestled on the slopes of the hill ranges. [Fig. 1, p. 26] There is hardly a straight line or border; the landscape is characterized by small, densely packed parcels of land which take on the form of the hill.

Through the analysis of the organization, the "idea," the "theme" for the potential design principle, was already encapsulated. Picture research can also provide a characteristic visual theme. There now follows a process of abstraction that serves to crystallize the elementary design principle. Abstraction means removing information step by step in order to eliminate the "more general." The derivation of the design principle is described in great detail in order to illustrate how actual conditions are translated into a visual principle. Considered more generally, what differentiates it from the process for static visual identities becomes clear: rather than a singular expression, one looks for a potential field that offers the widest range of networking opportunities. Another possibility is deriving the visual content from the development of word fields, as described in the Museion – Museum für moderne und zeitgenössische Kunst, Bozen case study, in which the visual identity it is not merely organized around a field

visual are continuous. Any form can pass over into any other. Any form of movement (a bird's flight for example) is a process of continuously changing forms, only in this case the change is 'fluid.' It is because any movement can be resolved back into single forms = phases that the film is possible: it consists of 24 static but continuous single pictures which, when projected, again create the illusion of movement." [18] Film is—technically speaking—a succession of individual images at a constant speed that is perceived as continuous motion. There are "given references" in continuous motion between two single images. However, film also provides the opportunity to cut up the continuum of motion and create new references. Thus, "given references" or "constructed, synthesized references" can exist between two single images, and provide a foundation for the compression and acceleration of motion and an important dramaturgical potential.

The video installation "24 Hour Psycho" by Douglas Gordon illustrates that the time-flow continuum and the single cut are complementary cinematic events. In this work, Hitchcock's

[18] Karl Gerstner, Designing Programmes, p.22.

"Psycho" is extended to a length of twenty-four hours. The prolongation of the takes before the unexpected murder, and the subsequent sequence of jump cuts during the murder are thus exaggerated. The slowing down is in fact what makes it possible to see the strobe-like cuts of the murder scene. The cuts are based on synthesized references between moments in time that actually have no direct temporal references, and yet through the continuous image motion we perceive them as interrelated. The narrative flow is based upon a continuous discon-tinuous sequence of images.

Contingency association

There are various processes for constructing references. Montage is one of them. A particularly poetic process that moves between continuity and discontinuity is that of metonymy: "A figure of speech in which a thing or concept is called, not by its own name, but by the name of something intimately associated with it" [19] — e.g. "to drink a glass." If a sentence is seen as a relatively solid structure made up of individual elements whose syntax and semantics can be related to each other, the figure of metonymy replaces one of these elements. The two swapped elements have a special relationship which Roman Jakobson calls an "elective affinity relationship": "The narrative moves from object to an adjacent one on paths of space and time or of causality; to move from the whole to the part and vice versa is only a particular instance of this process." [20] In his collection of essays "Poetik," Jakobson traces the "association by contiguity" in the work of the Russian writer Boris Pasternak. He demonstrates the process that enables a writer to convey a thought indirectly and only suggestively with an image from the Charlie Chaplin film "A Woman of Paris." In the film, the arrival of a train is shown through the reflections of light on the bodies of the passengers waiting on the platform. The effect takes the place of the cause — what creates and what is created, and the relationship that they have to one another, are conveyed in the same measure. The train travels past on screen, unseen by the audience, but something that emanates from it transforms its absence, making us conscious of it at the same moment.

[19] Alfred Hix Welsh, Studies in English Grammar, p. 222. [20] Roman Jakobson, Marginal Notes on the Prose of the Poet Pasternak, p. 310.

of free associations, but of precise lines of argument which repeatedly veer towards a central concept, namely to that of "passage."
It is crucial that in each type of derivation the central concept —
the "idea" — is open, open to various forms of expression, formats,
and media. The central concept and the basic theme enable a
medium-specific use of the visual identity across diverse media,
which translates into a stabilizing influence for the visual identity
that goes beyond a mere fashionable effect. The design principle
or the basic theme is the constant behind which is concealed
the "idea," the lynchpin of the visual identity that gives it substance. It represents the "rule" on the basis of which the variable
factors can "come into play." When the organization and its context, contents, and their visualization are interrelated, the visual
identity fulfills an important criterion for a fully developed flexible
visual identity.

Seen from a distance and from the air — and here is the first
abstraction step — an organic area like a patchwork is produced
by the fields. [Fig. 2, p. 26] Amongst these fields live the Rwandan
farmer families in traditional scattered settlements. Their huts
fit very naturally into the tapestry of fields and winding paths.
They are not disruptive factors but are protectively surrounded
by the landscape. The second stage of abstraction consists in
removing the color and increasing the contrast until a bitmap-like
representation emerges, supported by an additional rendering
into a black and white surface. [Fig. 1, p. 27] An observation —
namely the way in which the huts are integrated into the structure
of the landscape — is the key to the design principle and at the
same time the third abstraction step. The principle is based upon
the fact that the landscape is represented by organic forms and
the buildings by geometrical forms. [Figs. 2–3, p. 27]
The color spectrum of the Kigali Convention Center is as a whole
very wide, but certain color combinations are characteristic and

Figs. 1–2, p. 26; figs. 1–4, p. 27:
Kigali Convention Center (project
reference)

Visual identity by Axel Steinberger, Claudia
Wildermuth, Daniela Valentini, Jan-Eric
Stephan, Klaus Fromherz, and Ruedi Baur,
Integral Ruedi Baur, Zurich

are rendered through four specific colors derived from traditional fabric patterns. The color spectrum indirectly supports the elementary base. [Figs. 3–4, p. 27] **Greater significance is achieved through the defined combinations of certain colors than through individual colors or a group of individual colors.**
The "vocabulary"— style, color spectra, typefaces, textures, materials — forms the sign family on the basis of which the specific means of communication are designed. **The design principle is the basis of every implementation, and depends on the fact that a sign is surrounded, flowed around; for example, by a line. The direction of the flow is specified by the form of the sign. The sign is mostly the main information carrier: a typeface, abstracted architecture, or objects.** [Fig. 4, p. 27] **The way in which the hatchings lie around the sign is reminiscent of graphic processes such as woodcut. It is crucial for the design principle that the hatchings, textures, or color segments flowing around the sign assume a wave-like form. The variable aspects, the variation potentialities, lie in what the flowing around accomplishes: segment-like areas reminiscent of the parcels of land, circles similar to mosaics, etc. The principle is expressed in differentiated ways according to the diverse communication media: in three-dimensional implementations** [Fig. 2, p. 35: model of the congress center] **it becomes landscape; in two-dimensional implementations an abstracted (aerial) picture or plan. The design principle can be fundamentally translated into various media, signifier forms, dimensions, and rendering techniques. It enables every implementation—basic logo, typographical application, three-dimensional space — to reflect the principle in its media-specific way. The principle in itself is not enough; rather it is the imagination of the designer and the ability to evoke the potentialities that create the diversity in the variations. Only the initial steps can be described here; the designer, his talent for invention and trans-**

mission, and his style determine a considerable part of the development of a visual identity. Naturally, there are teammates who
participate in the game and its rules: graphic designers who implement the visual identity, and even future recipients, who keep
the visual identity alive with their improvisational and interpre-
tative joy.

Already in this first phase, this approach differs from that of the
development of static visual identities with singular logos. While
both working processes begin with an analysis of the organization / company, the results are interpreted in different ways.

According to the classic rules for static visual identities, from the
results of the analysis a "target state" is formulated that expresses
the target idea that deliberately contrasts with reality. "From
critical analysis of the 'actual', criteria and aims for an aspired-to
'target' gradually develop and are formulated. This 'target' can
then be balanced, e.g. via a semantic profile, with the 'actual'.
The imagined idea and reality are often miles apart…. When the
jointly worked out targets are defined the first phase of the design
process begins, in which the design concept is checked for its
correctness and loading capacity on exemplary models." [21]

Fully-developed flexible visual identities orient themselves more
strongly on "now." They convey current contents of the organization and its context, as described in chapter IV.

In the second phase of the development of static visual identities,
it is mainly a question of the definition of visual constants.
"Analogue to the components of a visual identity, the basic elements (name, logo, typeface, layout, etc.) are first specified and
applied to the elementary media (letterheads, business cards,
image brochures, internet, building signage, exhibition design)."
[22] In the specialist literature, there is little to be read about how
the designer arrives at the "basic elements to be specified."
In the case of visual identities of museums, it is, for example,

[21] Michael Klar, Das Ganze ist mehr als die Summe seiner Teile, in: Kompendium Corporate Identity und
Corporate Design, p. 26. [22] Josephine Prokop, Museen—Kulturschöpfer und ihre Markenidentität, p. 121.

architectural features that are translated into a sign, such as the Centre Georges Pompidou logo by the designers Jean Widmer and Ernst Hiestand, or the logo of the Museum of Contemporary Art in Tokyo – Watari-Um by the designer Ryoichi Kondo. In other cases, attributes shape the initial position: "The CD of Wolfsburg AG [23] should express modernity, international character, competence, and trustworthiness." [24] Wolfgang Schmittel writes, "A graphic solution should convey elegance, an impression of effortlessness, retentiveness, timelessness, and simplicity." [25] "Basic geometrical forms" are perceived as timeless: they have "brand value, their signal effect is familiar." [26] If the analysis has a one-sided focus on the formulation of attributes, the danger exists that the visual identity will be too unspecific, too general, or even cliché. This aspect will be dealt with in further detail in chapter IV.

In contrast, in this phase for fully developed visual identities, elements such as logo, typeface, or colors are not specified, but rather a design principle or basic theme that is open to implementation in several forms of expression, dimensions, formats, and media. Otherwise, from the beginning elements and their variations are assigned, such as the characters in the visual identity of Cité Internationale Universitaire de Paris: a group of foreign characters from other writing systems is assigned to each letter, and in the use of the visual identity are permutated, i. e. shifted around into all possible sequences. Thus they must be constituted in such a way that allows them to enter into all potential associations.

What is seen here in a specific case can be transferred onto a larger framework, such as the translation of a basic theme or design principle into another medium. The basic theme or design principle must be constituted in such a way that it can respond to the conditions of the particular other medium, and can "con-

[23] The corporate design was developed by wirDesign GmbH, Braunschweig. [24] Rayan Abdullah and Roger Hübner, Corporate Design (CD), p. 71. [25] Wolfgang Schmittel, Process Visual: Development of a Corporate Identity, p. 31. [26] Ibid.

nect with it." The same applies to the specific place and time context. The basic theme or design principle must be open enough so that, with its variations, it can have a specific message, and yet the overall visual identity remains recognizable. How can all these criteria be fulfilled simultaneously? In the following chapters we examine various possibilities such as module and building block, structure and permutation, and the "elemental."

The third phase is the specific implementation of the visual identity in which situation-specific variations are created. With static visual identities, the devised singular logo is, for the most part, obstinately applied like an appendage to all means of communication — irrespective of the specific contentual situation, and irrespective of whether they appear on printed matter, on the Internet, or as part of a signage system. To what extent the other instruments beside the logo — typographic features, color, or visual language — can relate to the concrete situation and the specific communication medium depends on how strictly their application is regulated.

With fully developed flexible visual identities, this step is connected to a variation, indeed a transformation. The design principle, the basic theme, or the "elemental" is translated into the appropriate communication medium in the form of expression suitable for the specific contentual matter. On this point, great differences in process can be observed in the visual identities discussed in this investigation. They range from examples in which the constant and variable are "merely applied," to others in which, although the design elements are fixed, the particular implementation for the continually updated state of the design is controlled by a computer program. Among these examples are the visual identities of Walker Art Center, Cité Internationale Universitaire de Paris, Flughafen Köln-Bonn, and the Twin Cities.

The typeface of the Twin Cities visual identity is modeled on current wind and temperature readings and thus creates — tongue in cheek — a playful relationship to reality.

Will such visual identities also remain an exception in the future? How is approaching a changing reality with design means even possible? How can changing forms of expression, language-like or even processual visual identities fulfill the classic requirements of static visual identities, according to which a visual identity stands out through repetition, simplicity, and signal effect? Is it conceivable that Karl Gerstner's pretension will be realized, and "the whole design becomes a signet"? Will a logo then be needed at all? The following chapters are devoted to these questions, and especially chapter IV, which also discusses their mode of action in critical contrast to static visual identities.

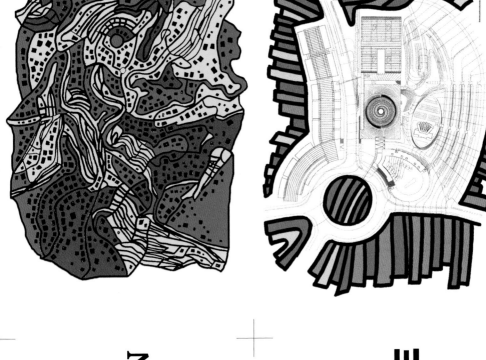

RWANDA
KIGALI
CONVENTION
CENTER

RWANDA
KIVU LAKE
HOTEL

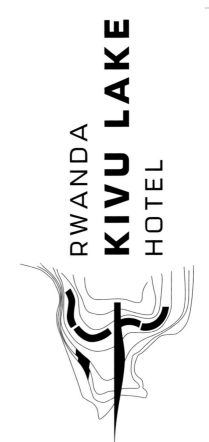

CN 22

CUSTOMS DECLARATION
DÉCLARATION EN DOUANE

Important! See instructions

May be opened officially
Peut être ouvert

Great Britain\Grande-Bretagne

Commercial sample\Echantillon

Gift\Cadeau

Other\Autre

Tick one or more

Documents

Quantity and detailed description of contents (1)
Quantité et description détaillée du contenu

Strc

Weight (in kg)(2) Poids
1.8k

Total Value (7)

Total Weight

For commercial items only

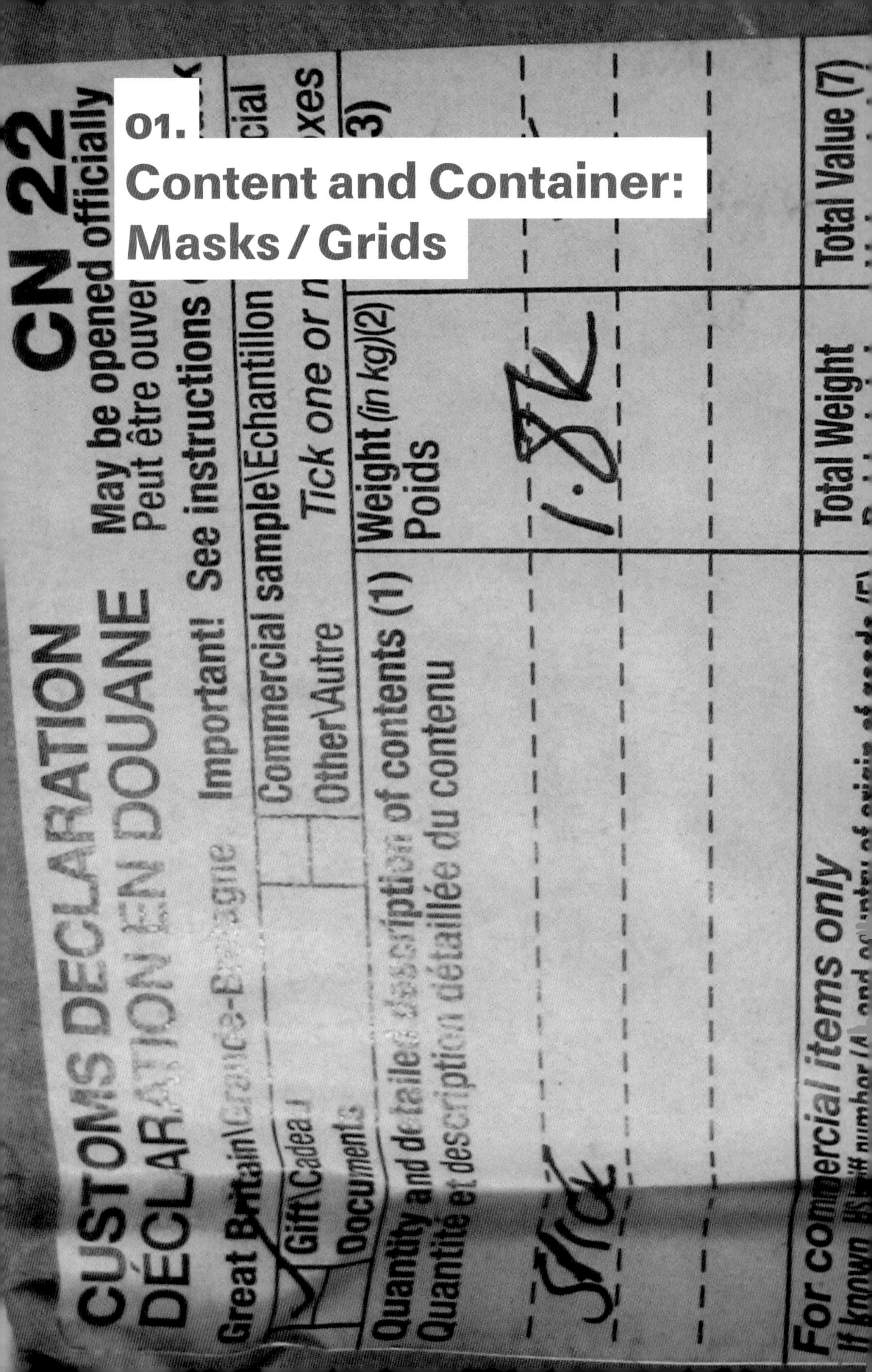

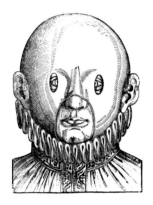

When can the visual identity of an organization be described as flexible? The boundary between static and flexible is rather fluid. There are many visual identities that function with a spectrum of colors that give rise to an element of variability. Among the first visual identities with this feature was the corporate design of Olivetti, designed by Hans von Klier in the 1960s, that worked with nine distinct colors. The advancement towards actual variability, however, is taken only when a constant factor interacts with a variable factor, when constants and variables combine in a sign or a family of signs.

The following chapter presents examples of simple variations created with masks or grids. In the visual identity of 2000 en France, the principle of the mask is applied to a single, logo-like element. The form's perimeter represents the constant, while the interior space is reserved for variable content. Alternately, a grid facilitates the systematic combination of several elements. A variable grid system is described using the example of "Ffm Lounge," a compilation of tracks by Frankfurt-based lounge musicians. With Ile Seguin-Rives de Seine, we see how a grid is particularly well suited for conveying complex information about transformative processes over an extended period of time.

Fig. 1, p. 36: Formulas specify text fields for specific entries, thus simplifying the processing of related content. The example of the fictive visual identity "Contains Multilingual Typography" uses a stable structure as a constant that can be filled with variable information.

Fig. 1, p. 37: Mask for correcting squinting

2000 en France
(Case Study 01)

"2000 en France" was the program title of the millennium celebrations in France organized by the Mission pour la célébration
de l'an 2000. Very distinct events organized throughout the
country were advertised with an overall visual identity. Special
events were also scheduled, such as a lecture series, open to
the general public, with internationally renowned scientists, the
UTLS – Université de tous les savoirs. The lecture series continued
beyond the celebrations for the year 2000 and is still ongoing.
"The theme of the project is the breaking up of ideas, of mix, blend,
diversity, globalization, the relationship between the real and
the virtual. Through its use by large organizations to local initia-
tives the various communication media represent a kind of survey
of graphic design in France." [01]

The constant figure of the visual identity is a filled circular area—
a symbol for the terrestrial globe — supplemented by several lines
of text that move around the circle in the form of a vortex. This
vortex represents what the year 2000 could be: an immaterial
layer of information connecting and reminding us of the Earth's
atmosphere. The vortex-shaped layout triggers a sensation of
movement in the sign. Because the type size becomes smaller
towards the center, an additional spatial effect is created between
text and circle. In the majority of cases, the title "2000 en France"
is a fixed part of the text.
This circle is the basic element; the outer limit of its shape represents the constant. Because of its reduced and elementary form,
the circle opens up a vast playing field for the designers who
adapted the visual identity to the various event venues in France.
The circle can be filled in a variety of ways, such as with colors,
structures, or photographs. Simple graphic motifs reinforce the
emblematic character [e. g., fig. 4, p. 39]; more complex, more
colorful motifs produce a strong dissolution effect [e. g., figs. 3

[01] Ruedi Baur, Ruedi Baur …, intégral…, and partners, p. 40.

and 5, p. 39]; and the swirling form of the mask can be further accentuated with an appropriate image [fig. 3, p. 40]. The texts— set in the Meta and Officina fonts — also assume various forms; in some versions its resolution is actually effectuated inside the circle. En-twirled by a wide variety of texts about the respective events, the emblem acts as a window opening up to diverse views.

Fully developed flexible visual identities convey their message through content, the consistent aspects of superordinate content, as well as variable customized content. Participating designers express in text and image their own ideas about the world and the future. While the masking functions as a norm guaranteeing constant recognition, it also frees up space for the individual designers' creative expression.

Visual identity by Eva Kubinyi and Ruedi Baur, Intégral Ruedi Baur et associés (www.integral.ruedi-baur.eu); in collaboration with Elise Muchir, Séverine Morizet, Gregor Stäuble, and Michelle Gubser. Project period: 1997–2000

Unique yet still commen- surable

This poster series created for an exhibition at Burg Giebichenstein, Hochschule für Kunst und Design Halle, was a joint study project in the fields of interior design and fine art. "Where does a feeling for one's home country begin, where does it end? In our view this feeling is something very personal that is nevertheless seen as something collective. Charms of the landscape, language, and tradition are connecting elements that determine our common concept of our home country. As strong as these vertices may be, different people always bring them together into an individual overall picture. Every single poster of this series for an exhibition concerned with the concept of home country is just as individual — various posters from tour operators and tourist information offices overprinted with information about an event." [02] Because the overprint has a stamp-like constancy, the poster variations, in spite of their different motifs, are identifiable as referring to the same event; and because of its transparency, subtle distinctions are perceptible in the changing backgrounds.

Poster series by Stefan Adlich (www.adlich.de)

Year of origin: 2004

Fig. 1, p. 42; figs. 1-2, p. 43: "Heimat" (Home) poster series

[02] Stefan Adlich, personal interview, 2008.

C

omroep voor kunst en cultuur

Lid worden is zo geregeld

C web-TV

Rize
Lorem ipsum dolor sit amet,
consectetuer adipiscing. Lorem ipsum
dolor sit amet, consectetuer adipiscing.

> Meer TV programma's

C web-radio

Programma titel
Lorem ipsum dolor sit
amet, consectetuer
adipiscing.

**Lorem ipsum dolor sit
amet**
Lorem ipsum dolor sit

Lorem ipsum
Lorem ipsum dolor sit
amet, consectetuer
adipiscing.

> Meer radio-programma's

C nieuws

Nieuws item titel
08-08-2006 - Lorem
ipsum dolor sit amet,
consectetuer adipiscing
elit. Integer sem
pede. Pellentesque blandit sem,
> Lees meer

Nieuws item titel
05-08-2006 - pede. Pellentesque blandit,
diam ac accumsan vehicula.
> Lees meer

Nieuws item titel
07-07-2006 - pede. Pellentesque blandit,
diam ac accumsan vehicula.
> Lees meer

> Meer nieuws

Nieuwsbrief

> Meer nieuws

C heeft de sympathie en
medewerking van o.a.:

CNO

omroep voor kunst en cultuur

omroep voor kunst en cultuur

→ Word lid!
→ C nieuws
→ Nu op C
→ Over C
→ Links

→ C gids
→ C agenda

Zoek

C Broadcasting

C is a Dutch broadcasting company specializing in the arts and culture. The visual identity is principally used in campaigns with which the company aims to gain more subscribers. The development of the visual identity involved creating the name "C" and the design of a series of logo variations. The letter "C" is displayed in various typefaces; e. g., with both serif and sans serif fonts. It is treated like a mask behind which various printed papers appear. In addition, techniques such as overprinting and the mixing of colors and structures were used.

Visual identity by Studio Dumbar (www.studiodumbar.com). Year of origin: 2006

Ffm Lounge
(Case Study 02)

"Ffm Lounge" is a compilation of tracks by lounge musicians, artists, and producers from Frankfurt encompassing various electronic and acoustic musical styles such as ambient and chill-out suitable as background music for cafés and bars. "Ffm Lounge" emphasizes its local origins but is designed as an expandable concept.

"Future releases for different cities are planned. It was important to create a unique word mark, which would allow the resident to identify with the product. In the case of Frankfurt Lounge it got shortened to 'Ffm Lounge.' In the case of Barcelona the compilation would be named 'Bcn Lounge.' The significant, but still flexible graphical language makes recognition very easy. Not just the recognition between different compilations from the same series, but as well as the recognition between product and advertisement." [03]

"The grid ... is ... (almost) inexhaustible as a programme." [04]
In the visual identity of "Ffm Lounge," the system of rules is the basis from which the variations are developed. Differentiation occurs within the area formed by the typography. The typeface designed for "Ffm Lounge" was also constructed out of a grid. The surface can appear monochrome and structured. The semitransparencies, resolution into patterns, and overprinting of colors make the aesthetics processual, and the development steps can be followed on the website. [05] The grid itself is visible only in some versions.

Visual identity by Martin Lorenz for HORT (www.hort.org.uk), currently at
www.twopoints.net. Year of origin: 2005

[03] Martin Lorenz, www.designby.twopoints.net/ffmlounge.php.   [04] Karl Gerstner, Designing Programmes, p. 16.   [05] www.frankfurt-lounge.com.

Ile Seguin-Rives de Seine

(Case Study 03)

The Ile Seguin-Rives de Seine quarter in Paris is a building site, a "spatium" (space) in the true sense of the word. The old "industrial town" — a Renault factory — ceased production in 1992 and was nearly completely demolished. The land was sold to the municipality in order to build a new district with residential and commercial buildings and offices. During the approximately ten-year construction process, a communication system has represented the not-yet-existing new town. It shows what is coming not in terms of single idealized images, but through a sequence of variable information about developments and activities.

In this visual identity, the grid also represents the constant system of rules. It enables four different levels of information to be distinguished within a design principle. Among these levels is information relating to (a) the overall project, meaning the development in general, and (b) the specific construction progress in the respective districts. In addition there is (c) information about the construction companies and sponsors involved, and (d) official announcements. As in a real city, the needs of those involved are quite diverse, and the demands made of communication design are high. Four visual languages convey these various levels of information. The language for the public announces the construction plans; the language for private investors advertises property for the future; and the internal language of the construction site itself ensures that it functions properly. Finally, there is another language—that of memory. In some places, new events write themselves like a palimpsest over the past: through the use of monochrome, transparent framed surfaces, the information level resembles a second skin that only partially covers the typographic logo and old wall fragments. The whole construction site is delimited by a barrier on which the name of the area, Ile Seguin-Rives de Seine, is overlaid in large letters. The lettering

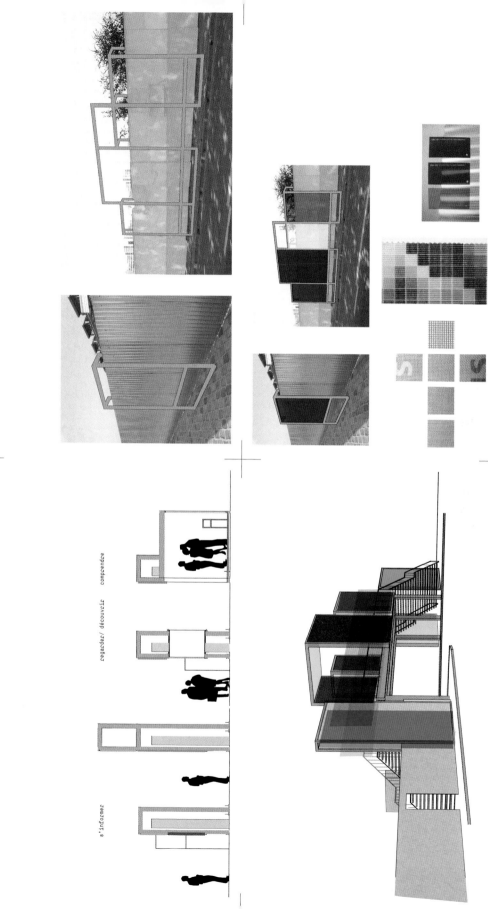

s'informer

regarder / découvrir

comprendre

accompanies visitors on their way around the site and implies
the consistent identification of the localities. [Fig. 1, p. 51] It forms
a latent narrative thread that is supplemented with a modular
frame system at strategically important points. The frame-grid
system is divided into various types that are different in size and
function: information boards with or without superstructures;
windows and openings facilitating inspection; and communication boxes depicting complex connections that can be used as
media terminals. In addition, the frame-grid system enables the
classification of individual investors. The most wide-ranging
visual elements can be fitted into the frames as in the grid of a
magazine. It is "the shot" that captures various moments: the
images illustrate the process of architectural development while
simultaneously informing future residents about the progress
of construction.

Visual identity by Ruedi Baur, Stéphanie Brabant, and Olivier Duzelier,
Intégral Ruedi Baur et associés, Paris; in collaboration with Sylvie Barrau,
Anatome. Year of origin: 2006

Figs. 1–3, p. 50: The original wall fragments are to be preserved (project
reference).

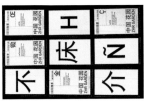

容那 多种语言 排字情形
CONTAINS MULTILINGUAL TYPOGRAPHY

214

EINFLUSS AUF
Kanji, Hiragana, Katakana, Hanja

MORPHEMSCHRIFT
Ein Schriftzeichen repräsentiert grundsätzlich ein Morphem. Verschiedene Morpheme mit der gleichen Lautstruktur werden durch verschiedene Zeichen wiedergegeben. Chinesisch ist somit die einzige heute noch gebräuchliche Sprache, die nicht primär auf Lautung einer Sprache zur Graffeel, sondern im Kern Mehrheit seiner Zeichen auch semantische Elemente trägt.

RADIKALE
Im ältesten chinesischen Lexikon aus dem Jahr 121 n. Chr. werden die Schriftzeichen nach einem System von Elementarfeldchen. Im sog. radikalen, eingeteilt. Diese Klassifizierung der Schrift nach Radikalen hat sich bis heute erhalten - 214 an der Zahl.

LOGOGRAMM
Die chinesische Schrift besteht vorwiegend aus Logogrammen. Im allgemeinen ist einem Zeichen ein Wort oder ein Partikel der chinesischen Sprache zugeordnet.

GESPROCHEN
Die chinesische Schrift wird vorwiegend zur Schreibung des Hochchinesischen verwendet. In China und Singapur in der vereinfachten Kurzzeichen-, in Taiwan noch in der traditionellen Langzeichen-Form.
Daneben dient die verwendete Schrift aber auch der Schreibung anderer chinesischer Sprachen. 1,2 Milliarden Menschen sprechen chinesisch.

GESCHICHTE
Die chinesische Schrift ist über 3000 Jahre alt. Die ältesten bisher gefundenen chinesischen Schriften sind in Orakelknochen und Schildkrötenpanzer eingeritzte Bildzeichen aus der Zeit um 1600 v.Chr. Bis zum Ende der Kaiserzeit wurde die chinesische Schrift vorwiegend zum Schreiben der klassischen Schriftsprache verwendet, die nur einer gebildeten Elite verständlich war. Seitdem wird die chinesische Schrift vorwiegend zum Schreiben der Hochchinesischen Sprache eingesetzt, die grammatisch den modernen nördlichen Dialekten ähnelt und von den Sprechern südlicher chinesischer Sprachen erlernt werden kann (mit welcher Aussprache auch immer). als Überregionales Medium der Verständigung. Als Kulturexport gelangte die chinesische Schrift etwa vor 600–800 n.Chr. auch in Nachbarländer und wird bis heute noch Südkoreas (Hanja) und Japan (Kanji, Hiragana, Katakana) als Teil der nationalen Schriftsysteme genutzt. Seit Beginn der Lateinisierungsbewegung in China wird versucht, explizit jedem Zeichen ein Laut zuzuordnen.

中国
CHINESE

INSTITUT FOR MULTILINGUAL TYPOGRAPHY. FIELD. AUSTELLUNGSTRASSE 60. 8005 ZURICH
WWW.INSTITUTFORMULTILINGUALTYPOGRAPHY.COM

ZHR
214

WHATEVER DESIGN OR MULTILINGUAL STYLES

7080
香港新生代
設計人展

香港參展設計師　國內參展設計師
區凱琳　柏志威，深圳
Au Hoi Lam　北邦，上海
Benny Iuk　陸國賢

ABCDEFG
HIJKLMN
OPQRSTU
VWXYZ

五专举五亩
们伵倰傸侁共
凤刺匇库屯
哂唱嗵圆垴

容年多种语言排字情形

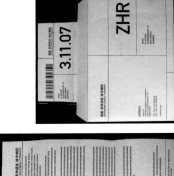

ZHR
3.11.07

容那 多种语言 排字情形

中国 花园
ZHR GARDEN
PAGE 2/2

3.11.07

容那 多种语言 排字情形

中国 花园
ZHR GARDEN

Contains Multilingual Typography

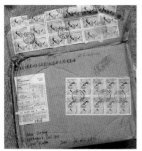

The fictive organization "Contains Multilingual Typography" is an exhibition space of cultures: "An institute dedicated to the aim of freeing languages from their isolation and mixing them with one another." [06] The basic element of the visual identity is a label reminiscent of a common cargo label, which communicates that the container transports valuable freight — language. "The cargo label contains information about the respective typographic system inside the container." [07] A defined layout of labels in which are anchored headers and footers as well as other fields of specified content has a stabilizing effect. The characteristic DIN font facilitates recognition. In each implementation, the label is filled in accordance with the specific information of the typographic system.

Visual identity by Jeannine Moser and Franziska Weissgerber. Created as part of the bachelor degree course in Visual Communication of the Department of Design, Zürcher Hochschule der Künste (ZHdK). Year of origin: 2007

Figs. 1-3, p. 53: Examples of various labels (project reference)

Serialize

Flexible visual identities may contain serial components in the design process and in their characteristics. In contrast to classically varying series, which typically develop in a chronological sequence, the variations of a flexible visual identity may also appear simultaneously, in different communication media, and/or in different loca-

tions. Examples of just such a series are the posters for the Schaubühne am Lehniner Platz in Berlin, in which the only constant is the typographic logo. The second distinguishing sign of the Schaubühne, the "zeit.genossen-Kreis-säge" (contemporary circular saw), is included in the design context as a constant/variable sign, varying not only in color, but also in signification. For example, while in the poster for

the play "Gesäubert" it is incorporated into the lizard design, on other posters it serves as an abstract design focus. Project design by Heinrich Kreyenberg, heute-morgen, Büro für Gestaltung (www.heute-morgen.com). Project period: since 2002

Figs. 1-2, p. 54: Posters for the Schaubühne am Lehniner Platz, Berlin

Summary

Flexibility is created by the interplay between constant and variable elements. In the case studies described, either the container — the mask or the grid — is fixed and the content — the inner area—variable, or vice versa. 2000 en France demonstrates that a visual identity can acquire a coherent and characteristic expression even when various designers are involved in the process. The constant container provides space that designers use in their own way. Various figures can be created on the basis of a system of rules — such as a grid — which are related to each other in their shape, size, and proportions, and which can be varied, such as in the color scheme. A grid is hardly suitable as the sole feature of a visual identity, but it can form its characteristic foundation. In the visual identity of "Ffm Lounge," the typography is constructed on a grid. Whether the grid is concretely depicted or not, it remains recognizable as a design basis. In the example of "Contains Multilingual Typography," the fields of the grid specify in what position a certain type of content is to be found, and at the same time the field is linked to a certain design. This example shows that a structure, a specified arrangement of content, can form the constant. The constant generates an opportunity for comparison that allows the differences between the writing systems to be recognized.

The visual identity for Ile Seguin-Rives de Seine illustrates how various contents — the four languages — can be set in relationship to each other with a grid. Variable content retain their "Gestalt" (form) over a long period of time with a fixed frame or a grid which, in the case of the Ile Seguin-Rives de Seine construction site, enables visitors to follow changing activities within a long-term process on a continuing basis.

02.
Element and Sequence: Movement / Change of Perspective

This chapter deals with the representation of movement diversely manifested in visual identities: as animation, a pulsing structure, an illustrated or photographic sequence, and as a snapshot— two-dimensional or three-dimensional.

By means of single "stills" directly generated from movement, movement's characteristics can be translated back into graphic representation. This process can be seen in the logo variations of the visual identity of EXPO Hannover, in which one can discern an alternation between concentrated sign and dissolving texture. In the visual identity of Lakeside Science & Technology Park, movement is depicted by means of eleven different calligraphic signatures in a sign reminiscent of a typographic element or a dancing figure. Finally, the visual identities of the Kunsthaus Graz and the Cinémathèque française will be explored in terms of the representation of spatial movement.

Fig. 1, p. 56: "Varied patterns (inter-ference) arise when waves coming from different directions meet and mingle." [01]

[01] Theodor Schwenk, Sensitive Chaos, p. 141.

EXPO 2000 Hannover

(Case Study 04)

EXPO 2000 Hannover was the first world's fair in Germany and took place from June 1 to October 31, 2000. More than 170 nations exhibited their view of the future under the motto, "Man, Nature and Technology." In comparison to previous world's fairs, the concept was fundamentally redefined: EXPO 2000 was not only comprised of exhibitions of technical achievements, but also provided a platform for global dialogue on the key themes of the twenty-first century.

The constant of the visual identity is a perpetually mutating "impulse," which is simultaneously the variable. It symbolically conveys the dynamic processes of EXPO 2000 and represents the aim of reacting flexibly to future developments without losing identity in the process. [02]

The form of the impulse is constantly changing, a metamorphosis conveyed in print media through various "fixed images," or elsewhere as real animation. The wide range of colors — there are 456 defined color combinations — contribute to the highly variable nature of the visual identity. The movement of the impulse creates an "energy field" [03] that, with its moiré-like structure, alludes to digital photography and video technologies, while also citing traces of technical processes. Additionally, an implied reference is made, though not explicitly rendered, to scientific imaging such as infrared or false-color photography. The high-contrast signal colors and the consistent wordmark — "EXPO 2000 Hannover: The World Exhibition" — set in Franklin Gothic No. 2 form the antithesis to the flowing half-tone pattern-like impulse.

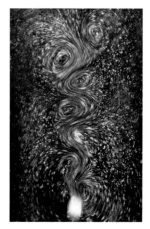

The quality of the impulse lies not only in its dynamics, but also in the fact that, without a fixed delimitation, it flitters between sign and structure, as either of the two forms dominates in its diverse representations. Whereas it appears on the Inter City

Fig. 1, p. 58: Despite the hardness of the wood, the trunk of an olive tree has a whirl-shaped grain.

Fig. 2, p. 58: "A suitable duration of exposure has revealed something of the structure of a train of vortices. A meandering stream winds its way between the separate vortices." [04]

[02] See Michael Gais and Iris Utikal, unpublished manuscript, n. pag. [03] Ibid.
[04] Theodor Schwenk, Sensitive Chaos, p. 142.

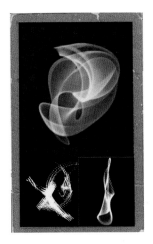

Express Train [fig. 1, p. 61] **as a rather limited, signal-like sign, on the façade of the Expo-Café** [fig. 4, p. 61] **it appears as texture. And while in some manifestations it stands out colorfully from the background, in others it blends into it more completely. Over its six years of development, the visual identity gave way to variations of a broad spectrum that "very much corresponds to the nature and basic conceptual idea of the impulse: imploding and exploding, a fluent change of dimension and thereby a visualization of change and process in the best sense."** [05] **The dissolution into texture makes the impulse literally processual. Continually regenerating its "Gestalt" (form) like a vortex or a swirl, the silhouette represents something flowing, a transition with the subtlest shadings; without sharp contours, the surfaces fade into the background as a pattern of halftone dots. Seen in this way, this visual identity diverges in several respects from classic design rules, according to which a logo should stand out though simplicity, clarity, uniformity, and its distinctive nature. Nevertheless, or precisely because of it, the design of the impulse is quite memorable as the intensity of its iridescent colors draws one's attention.**

Visual identity by Michael Gais and Iris Utikal, QWER (www.qwer.de).

Project period: 1994–2000

Fig. 1, p. 59: In the 1950s, the artist Ben Laposky developed abstract figures with the help of oscilloscopes, electronic measuring devices for the visual presentation of independent electrical signal voltages.
The three illustrations show that vortices can be quite different yet still recognizable as vortices.

[05] Ibid.

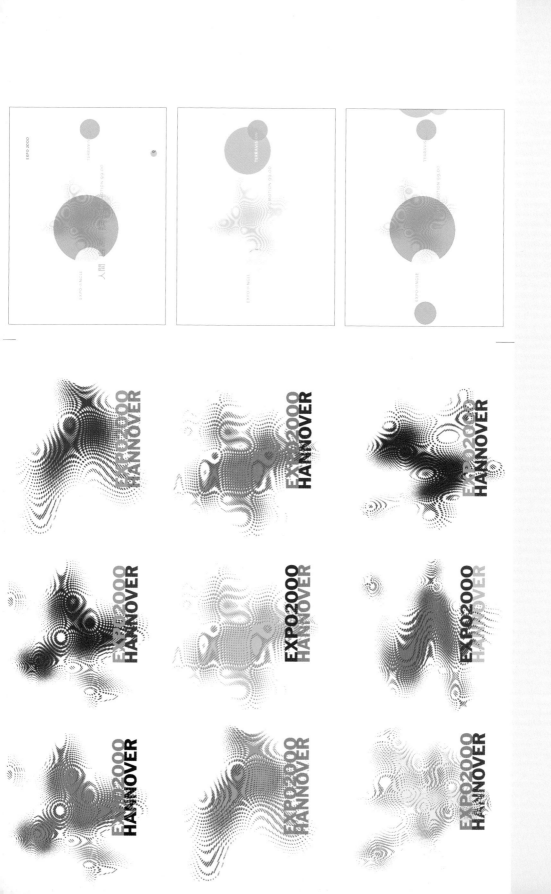

EXPO2000
HANNOVER

The World Exposition
Germany

Mankind Nature Technology

1 June – 31 October 2000

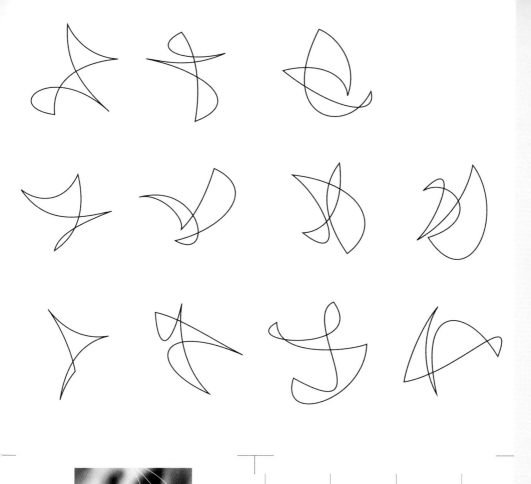

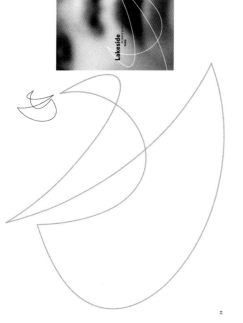

Lakeside
SCIENCE & TECHNOLOGY
PARK

01
Lakeside
SCIENCE & TECHNOLOGY
PARK

Lakeside
SCIENCE & TECHNOLOGY
PARK

02
Lakeside
SCIENCE & TECHNOLOGY
PARK

Lakeside
SCIENCE & TECHNOLOGY
PARK

04
Lakeside
SCIENCE & TECHNOLOGY
PARK

05
Lakeside
SCIENCE & TECHNOLOGY
PARK

Lakeside
SCIENCE & TECHNOLOGY
PARK

07
Lakeside
SCIENCE & TECHNOLOGY
PARK

08
Lakeside
SCIENCE & TECHNOLOGY
PARK

Lakeside
SCIENCE & TECHNOLOGY
PARK

10
Lakeside
SCIENCE & TECHNOLOGY
PARK

11
Lakeside
SCIENCE & TECHNOLOGY
PARK

Lakeside Science & Technology Park

(Case Study 05)

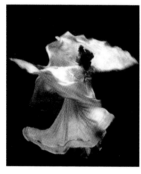

"Lakeside Science & Technology Park is located just a few hundred meters from Lake Wörthersee, directly neighbouring the University of Klagenfurt and upon completion will offer 28,000 m² of office space. Lakeside Park is a platform for cooperation between enterprises and university institutions in the information and communication technology (ICT) sectors. A place of interdisciplinary research and development, training, production and services. Companies and research institutions which share this thematic focus and are synergistically complementary are brought together here with an intention to cooperate in select R&D projects: a continual workshop of operational development and university research, with experts from business, technical fields and social sciences. With the goal of bringing innovative solutions into being; to present the world with 'the latest'." [06] "Energy is in movement. If the nature of cooperation is to be made visible, it is always a snapshot of a permanent process between at least two parts, participants or sharers.... Here it does not need a conventional emblem, no abbreviation to a visual cartridge for burning into (branding) the skin, the retina. Here it needs the visual significance of a moment of cooperative action made visible, it needs more than only 'one': one and one is eleven." [07]

The movement is symbolized by a calligraphic figure broken into various "snapshots," which form eleven logo variations. [Fig. 2, p. 64] The fonts DTL Prokyon, developed by Erhard Kaiser for the Dutch Type Library, and TEFF Collis, developed by Christoph Noordzij for Enschedé Font Foundry, provide the weighting of the three elements of the typographic logo: "Lakeside" is the dominant term to which the term "Science & Technology" is subordinated. [Fig. 3, p. 64] The color spectrum employed in the visual identity consists of nine colors, with blue and green dominant.

Figs. 1-2, p. 65: Most of the visual identities examined work with figures that move within themselves. They are comparable with dance-like figures, like Loie Fuller here, or bring to mind the movement of writing.

[06] Lakeside Science & Technology Park GmbH, www.lakeside-scitec.com/en.
[07] Clemens Theobert Schedler, unpublished manuscript, n. pag.

Continuity is also created by a recognizable design of the calligraphic figure: all eleven variants have the same line thickness,
take up the same area, and each consists of curves and sharp
angles intersecting at least once. They primarily appear two-
dimensional, but in connection with a photograph, optically the
line appears three-dimensional. [Fig. 4, p. 67] In some versions,
they blend back into one figure and appear to be truly animated.

Visual identity by Clemens Theobert Schedler, Büro für konkrete Gestaltung
(www.konkretegestaltung.at); in collaboration with Erhard Kaiser (font modifications and design of the calligraphic figure —"5th element"). Project period:
since 2003

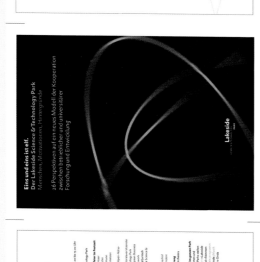

Kunsthaus Graz

(Case Study 06)

Kunsthaus Graz describes itself as "a multidisciplinary venue for exhibitions, activities and other means of presenting contemporary art, new media, and photography." [08] The building designed by the London architects Peter Cook and Colin Fournier provides an appropriate framework for its ambitious program. "The aesthetic dialogue between the new biomorphic structure on the bank of the Mur and the old clock tower on Graz's famous Schlossberg (Castle Hill) is the trade-mark of a city aiming to create a productive tension between tradition and avant-garde.... While the building's interior is meant to inspire its curators as a black box of hidden tricks (Colin Fournier), its outer skin is a media façade which can be changed electronically." The huge BIX screen developed by the architects reality:united, "gives the impression that not a screen but the Kunsthaus itself renders images and pictures." [09]

The constant element of the visual identity is derived from axes of coordinates — as used in a coordinate system — representing spatiality and orientation in space. [10] The figure is also an allusion to a construction element of the building, part of the "sub-skin" serving to coordinate various systems of exhibition operations including lighting, monitoring and alarm systems, exhibition construction systems, and loudspeakers. The system is not concealed but instead is "a discernible secondary constructive structure." [11] The visual identity is based on a constant singular logo: an axes of coordinates, which in some versions appears as a spatial animation. For example, on the website it reacts to a mouse click and floats freely over the surface of text and images. It is also used in animated form in a flipbook based upon the development process of the Kunsthaus as documented on a webcam. During the opening phase of the Kunsthaus, the logo was presented as a film on the BIX media façade.

Fig. 1, p. 68: "The right-hand rule is a common mnemonic for understanding notation conventions for vectors in 3 dimensions" (project reference). [12]

Fig. 2, p. 68: Element of the "subskin" of Kunsthaus Graz. The "subskin" is based on "a regular grid of connection points into which any modular connecting bars can be hung." [13] Thus each site is provided with data and energy.

[08] Kunsthaus Graz, www.kunsthausgraz.steiermark.at/cms/beitrag/10201227/4938704/. [09] Kunsthaus Graz, www.kunsthausgraz.steiermark.at/cms/ziel/4975814/EN/. [10] Lichtwitz, unpublished manuscript, n. pag. [11] See realities:united, www.realities-united.de. [12] http://en.wikipedia.org/wiki/Right-hand_rule; cited in Lichtwitz, unpublished manuscript, n. pag. [13] See realities:united, www.realities-united.de.

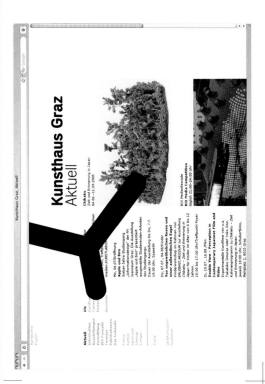

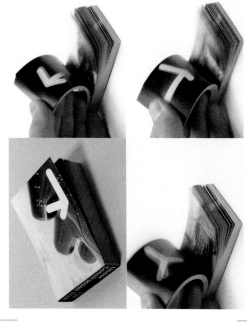

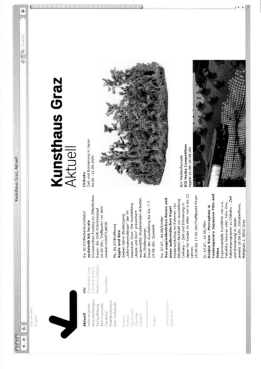

The implementations achieve their diversity mainly through the
representation of artworks, which come to the fore through the
reserved design. Often only typographical means are used. The
font was developed specifically for the Kunsthaus and shares
certain characteristics with the logo: lines with rounded ends and
uniform width. Instead of a dominant color scheme, contrasts are
created through various materials and surfaces, such as opaque—
transparent and matte — gloss. The use of logo variations — single
"stills" generated from the depiction of spatial movement — for
other communication media is also planned.

Visual identity by Kriso Leinfellner, Stefanie Lichtwitz, and Harald Niessner,
Lichtwitz (www.lichtwitz.com); in collaboration with Kasimir Reimann, Benedikt
Flüeler, Susanne Tobeiner (project coordination), and Hubert Jocham and
URW++ (font modifications). Year of origin: 2003

Cinémathèque française

(Case Study 07, Part 1)

The Phenomenological View

Seen phenomenologically, the various projection surfaces of the Cinémathèque point towards the infinite number of viewpoints that are contained within one view. Cinematographically, on the other hand, it is a matter of the object changing position. The Cinémathèque signs represent the ability to capture movement, as was seen for the first time in Muybridge's serial photographs. Therefore, they also represent the history of the invention of cinema, and, at the same time, refer to the magic of the moving picture. In both aspects there is both a historical dimension as well as a reference to modern-day film production. The systematically varying views of the table [fig. 4, p. 73] depict a fictive movement, though the shape of the object remains unchanged. Only the perspective changes, and it is relative to the position of the observer. When we perceive an object, we do so from an entirely designated side. "But this thing is not (merely) the side genuinely seen in this moment; rather (according to the very sense of perception) the thing is

The Cinémathèque française is a Paris film institute whose aim is the conservation of films, as well as props and costumes. Each year more than a thousand films are shown in their screening rooms. In September 2005, the Cinémathèque moved into new premises in the former American Center designed by the architect Frank O. Gehry. His architecture bears the hallmarks of deconstruction: the geometrical bodies appear distorted, twisted, and displaced, thus forming a dynamized whole. At night, discrete sections of the façade are illuminated by projected light areas and are thus transmuted into two and three-dimensional signs of the visual identity. A symbiotic relationship exists between the Cinémathèque building and its visual identity. Upon entering the building, the visual identity takes up the dynamics of the building exterior in the interior: the foyer presents itself as a lively play of light and shadow.

The visual identity is based on a constant signifier: a projection plane in the form of a bright rectangle with blurred edges. This projection plane varies in implementation for different media, a process discussed in chapter 3. The projection planes also are shown from different perspectives, a sequence giving the impression that an imaginary projector is being moved through the space, which, depending upon one's perspective, seems as if either the viewer or the projector itself is moving. In contrast to the representation of movement in the previously discussed visual identities, it appears as if it is not the object that is moving but the eye — or the projector — perceiving the movement.

Visual identity by Intégral Ruedi Baur et associés

LA CINÉMATHÈQUE FRANÇAISE

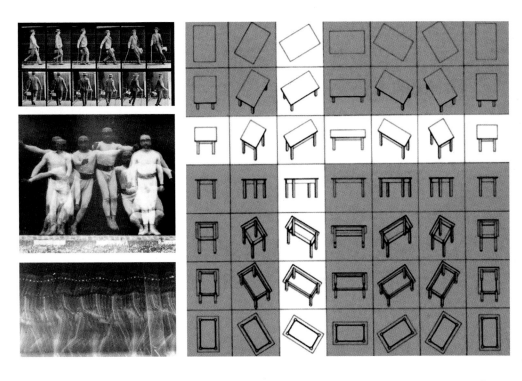

precisely the full-thing that has still other sides, sides that are not brought to genuine perception in this perception, but that would be brought to genuine perception in other perceptions." [14]
Perception is not restricted to individual perspectives but rather connected with a permanent change of perspective. In perception there is thus an interaction between "real exhibiting"

[15] of the object and "empty indicating that refers to possible new perceptions." [16]

Fig. 1, p. 73: Eadweard Muybridge's serial photographs show spatial movement. However, here it is not the camera that moves around a fixed object but vice versa: a series of cameras are in fixed positions and a person moves in front of them.

Figs. 2–3, p. 73: In contrast, in Étienne-Jules Marey's chrono-photographic depictions of sequences of movement, the movement can be seen within one single photograph.

Fig. 4, p. 73: Karl Gerstner visualizes Husserl's conceptual model by representing forty-nine systematically varying views of a table from above.

[14] Edmund Husserl, Analyses Concerning Passive and Active Synthesis, p. 40.
[15] Ibid., p. 41. [16] Ibid.

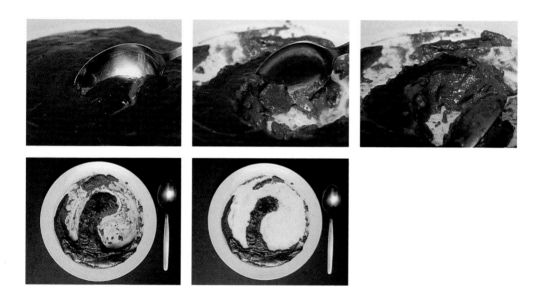

Deconstruction and Condensation

"It is important to capture moments, figuratively, textually, and collectively, in order to attempt to take up various positions in relation to them and understand the beginnings and possibilities of a process. There are many possibilities for capturing processes in images. Whether as a motion blur, relicts, traces in a single picture, as well as superimposing pictures, contrasts, and image sequences .... A growing pile of documents, rusting iron, a rising water level, and the sensuousness of sound are examples of material synonyms." [17]

Figs. 1–5, p. 74: With serial photography it is possible to bridge chronological and spatial distances so as to compare various conditions with each other. Here the series "Puddingessen" (Eating pudding) shows a visual analogy to the mining of brown coal from an open cast pit (project reference). [See Case Study 12: Ferropolis]

Figs. 1–5, p. 75: In these multiple exposures, time is not broken up into individual phases; rather, the single moments overlap and condense.

Photographic work by Bernhard Moosbauer (www.exsample.org)

     [17] Antje Reineck, unpublished manuscript, n. pag.

Summary

Since the 1990s, computer graphics programs have facilitated the large-scale development and rendering of animations. While the majority are logo-like signs, we also find sign-like textures. In the visual identity of EXPO 2000 Hannover, a dynamic is created as the sign strongly dissolves towards texture in some implementations, while in others it is once again condensed; i.e., its silhouettes take on a more delimited form. The form is always in the process of creation as it flitters between solid states. And yet, despite these transformations, its significant expression renders the "impulse" of EXPO 2000 recognizable, because the "Gestalt" (form), as Karl Gerstner says, remains unchanged — irrespective of whether the logo variation takes on a longer, more oval, or more circular shape. The characteristics of the design in this example are defined by its particular halftone dot-like texture and undulating appearance manifest in all of the variations.

The theme of "condensation and dissolution" is generally a very important aspect of the "processual," and is particularly apt for short-lived events where energies briefly converge.

The technical possibilities of animation have, retroactively, had a great influence on classic graphic design methodology, thus creating new means of graphic expression, which, for their part, can also be animated. In the visual identity of the Lakeside Science & Technology Park, the nine different calligraphic figures, like freeze frames of a dance movement, produce a coherent picture as the basic figure from which they are created remains consistently the same. Most of the visual identities examined work with figures that move within themselves. The Kunsthaus Graz logo, which also moves across a surface and thus changes its position, is an exception, which can be explained by the fact that changes in position and form are very complicated to represent. Variation through movement principally influences the sign's form, and because the form is one of the strongest aspects of a sign, its stability must be established through a recognizable "Gestalt" (form).

The motion aspect in the sign variation of the Cinémathèque française simulates the movement of a projector as it projects a plane of light, or the movement of a person who moves through the space and perceives the projection plane from different perspectives. For such graphic representation, the methods employed include blurring and gradient. The "projection as such" is emphasized by placing the variable perspective in relation to a fixed perspective.

To represent movement, one can employ techniques such as motion blurring, the superimposing of images, and picture sequencing. While no suitable visual identity could be found to represent this last technique, the picture sequence of the "Puddingessen" (Eating pudding) series provides an example.

03.
Theme and Variation:
Transformation

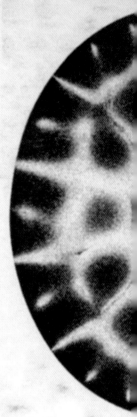

1   1021 Hertz.

Fig. 1, p. 78: "A special example of the 'Gestaltung' of an animal's appearance is the armor surface of a tortoise shell, which more often than not displays a coherent structure. The heart-shaped middle is divided into thirteen fields and is surrounded by a ring of twenty-four or twenty-five shield plates. At certain frequencies, the various oscillating forms in the basic structure of the tone figures of plates, ellipses, or cross-sectional areas of tortoise shells exhibit great similitude to the structural principles in the configuration of this animal's carapace: the edge with twenty-four fields and the clearly delineated middle section with five successive fields down the middle of the dorsal." [01]

How does one differentiate the various parts of an organization? How does one address a heterogeneous public in a targeted fashion? And how does one use the multiplicity of the contemporary media lexicon? In brief: How can visual signs and sign systems simultaneously create both coherence and variability? This chapter is about variation processes applied to singular signs. Various expressive features can be altered: shape, size, and color; degree of abstraction; and means of representation, i.e., communication media. Modifying the form, e.g., a change on the typographic level, is one of the more potent manners of transforming a sign, and is employed in the visual identities of the Frankfurter Kunstverein, the Museum Boijmans van Beuningen Rotterdam, and the Galerie für zeitgenössische Kunst, Leipzig. Furthermore, they create variations through various degrees of abstraction so that one and the same signified can appear as a reduced sign, as a typeface, and as a spatial configuration. This modification is demonstrated with the competition design for a visual identity for the Museion – Museum für moderne und zeitgenössische Kunst, Bozen, and the visual identity of the Kigali Convention Center. A change in medium represents a potent transformation for a sign family, as seen with the visual identities of the Cinémathèque française — examined in the previous chapter for its characteristic representation of spatial movement — and the Quartier des spectacles. The Beaux-arts de Paris case study shows how the different traces of complementary tools connect the level of representation with the level of production in the visual identity of an arts university.

[01] Alexander Lauterwasser, Wasser Klang Bilder, p. 62.

International Red Cross and Red Crescent Movement

The International Red Cross and Red Crescent Movement's mission is, "to protect human life and health, to ensure respect for the human being, [and] to prevent and alleviate human suffering, without any discrimination based on nationality, race, religious beliefs, class or political opinions." [02] The Red Crescent, recognized in 1929 as a protection symbol equivalent to the Red Cross on a white background — the reverse of the Swiss flag, is used to avoid offending religious sentiments of soldiers, and is also based on a reversal, in this case the flag of the Ottoman Empire. The symbols "Red Lion with Red Sun" and "Red Crystal" also serve as signs of organizations belonging to the Red Cross and Red Crescent Movement. The main function of visual identities is generally to represent an organization. In this case it is subordinated to the protective function. The protection symbols designate people and objects under the protection of international humanitarian law. The family of signs only appears as a whole for demonstration purposes, otherwise only one of the symbols is used. In comparison, sign families usually also appear spatially in parallel.

The "Red Crystal" was created by a design collective under the direction of François Bugnion, Director and Head of the Department of International Law and Communication (International Committee of the Red Cross). Year of origin: 2006

[02] http://en.wikipedia.org/wiki/Red_Cross.

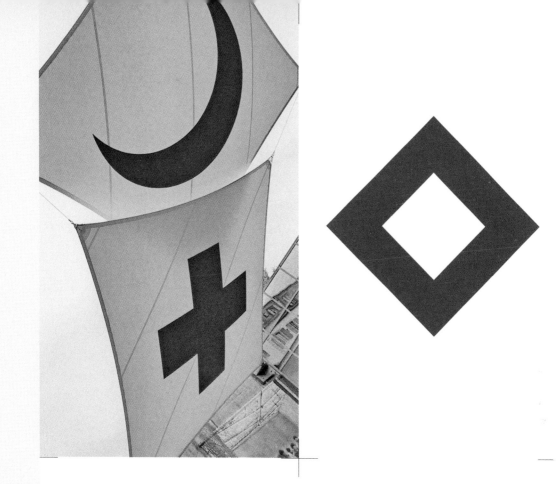

Dutch PTT

In 1989, the Dutch state-owned post and telecommunications company — PTT Posterijen, Telegrafie en Telefonie — was privatized and renamed KPN Koninklijke PTT Nederland. Later, in 1998, it was divided into the postal sector PTT Post (now TNT Post) and the telecommunications field KPN. The new visual identity — a logo family — was created in 1989 during the course of privatization, and includes various basic geometrical figures—circle, point, line, and square — arranged beside the singular logo on a grid. For internal use, such as on company stationary, the elements are employed uniformly. In other manifestations, such as on everyday objects like telephone boxes, vehicles, and buildings, they are set free and applied in a playful fashion.

Visual identity by Studio Dumbar. Year of origin: 1989

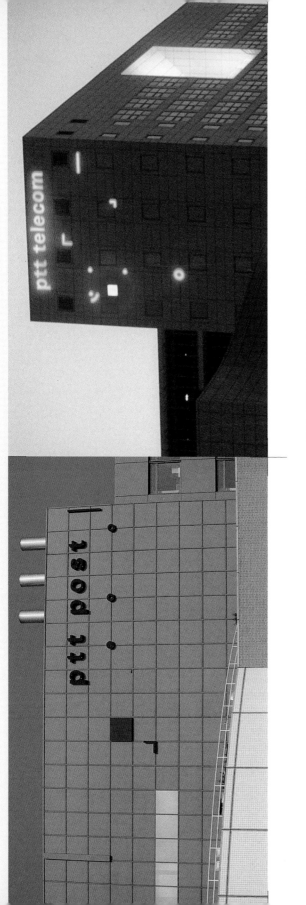

Frankfurter Kunstverein

(Case Study 08)

The Frankfurter Kunstverein describes one of its aims as follows:
"Our commitment is to elucidate the importance of the role of
artists in our society: as producers, thinkers, mediators and the
ones who still dare to experiment." [03] This also encompasses
the view of the organization's own identity and its visual communication. Director Chus Martinez characterizes the Frankfurter
Kunstverein as an institution permanently reinventing itself.

The visual identity of the Kunstverein represents an openness to
new ideas and projects about art and art education, an innovative attitude reflected not only on a symbolic level, but through
constant reinvention as the institution develops. Each part of the
Kunstverein is allocated its own sub-visual identity. Besides the
permanent features such as the exhibition and event platform, the
café, and the membership concept "10 Reasons to be a Member,"
this also applies to each new, temporary project. Each new project brings the development of another sub-visual identity, only
to disappear at the project's close.
In order to visualize sub-visual identities they must be highly
differentiated, and thus a particularly marked aspect must be
defined as a variable; a sign's form represents one of its more
distinguishing aspects. Since the differentiation of the various
parts of the Frankfurter Kunstverein is the prime consideration,
a wealth of forms can most easily be achieved by typographic
means, i.e., through contrasting fonts. These "should not so much
create harmony but also reflect the points of friction that present
themselves in the Kunstverein." [04] A color change, for example,
would be too weak as a main distinguishing feature and would
not produce sufficient contrast. Among the individual parts are
the exhibition platform, designed in the font Knockout; "Speaking
of Others," the area for artists' talks, in Caslon; and "10 Reasons
to be a Member" in Signpainter. The typeface of the café is set

[03] Frankfurter Kunstverein, www.fkv.de/frontend_en/ueber_uns.php.
[04] Sven Michel, personal interview, 2008.

in Fraktur and is a slightly ironic allusion to the historical sur-
roundings of the Kunstverein.

On compositions such as posters and brochures, several areas
are promoted at the same time. Here the distinction is supported
by means of montage. Overlaps, changes of direction, tilted
positions, and cropped elements create a heterogeneous overall
picture and avoid the impression that it is merely designed with
different fonts. These design principles produce coherence in the
overall visual identity, but particularly in the compositions. They
stand out for their very powerful, emphatic, almost raw style, and
thus also give the visual identity a processual effect.

Visual identity by Stefan Hauser, Laurent Lacour, and Sven Michel; with David
Jalbert-Gagnier and Nicole Klein, ade hauser lacour (www.adehauserlacour.de).
Project period: since 2006

KAPITEL 1 „IST DAS LEBEN NICHT SCHÖN?"
GRUPPENAUSSTELLUNG IN 4 KAPITELN

ESRA ERSEN, 5. APRIL – 5. JUNI 2006

FRANKFURTER KUNSTVEREIN

RESIDENCY PROGRAM

SPEAKING OF OTHERS

cafe im kunstverein

10 REASONS
TO BE
A MEMBER

FRANKFURTER KUNSTVEREIN

Frankfurter Kunstverein
Steinernes Haus am Römerberg
Markt 44
60311 Frankfurt am Main

Telefon +49.69.219314 - 0
Fax +49.69.219314 - 11
post@fkv.de / www.fkv.de

Graphic profile sponsored by
ade hauser lacour

Museum Boijmans van Beuningen Rotterdam
(Case Study 09)

The museum describes what it has to offer as extremely varie-
gated: "Museum Boijmans van Beuningen Rotterdam is an extremely many-sided museum. Wandering through its galleries
you will journey through the history of art, from the Middle Ages
until the present day. The collections are striking in their diversity, housing old master and modern paintings alongside product
design and the applied arts, and encompassing the full range of
media from painting and sculpture, prints and drawings to photography, video and film." [05]

Its visual identity is based on the interplay between firmly defined
and freely modifiable typographical elements. The singular logo
is not a detached, additional element, but part of "Boijman's font,"
based on a modification of the font designed by Lance Wyman
for the 1968 Olympic Games in Mexico. The more typical, Op Art-
inspired character of the font remains, and is supplemented by
capital letters, additional typefaces, and special characters.
In turn, the typeface indicates distinct hierarchies. [Fig. 2, p. 92]
The styles differ in the number of lines. All elements of the overall identity as well as the guidance system are designed with this
font. In contrast, each temporary exhibition is publicized with a
unique typographical solution evoking the prevailing theme and
subject matter. The publicity appears on two different panels,
outside and inside the museum's lobby, and coherence is created
between the two typographical levels through stylistic means.
The dynamic of the variable elements is further reinforced by the
makeshift impression created by the boards leaning up against
the wall.

Visual identity by Armand Mevis and Linda Van Deursen. Project period:
2002–2007

In Transition

There is a particular aesthetics of
transition experienced on building
sites, backstage areas, loading docks,
or in waiting rooms. Superordinate
coherencies disappear in favor of
unexpected constellations. The aesthetics of transition marks a characteristic stage within a process and
reveals itself in the traces left by different activities: stacking, layering,
bulk distribution. "The purpose of
allowing the panels to lean, rather
than attaching them to the wall, is to
communicate the idea of the museum
as a work in progress. On the day of
opening, the designers encountered
several visitors who believed that
they had arrived too early, before the
displays had been completed." [06]

[05] Museum Boijmans van Beuningen Rotterdam, www.boijmans.rotterdam.nl/en/5/many-sided-museum.
[06] Angus Hyland and Emily King, c/id: Visual Identity and Branding for the Arts, p. 113.

Rondom Dürer

Duitse prenten en tekeningen ca 1420–1575

RIRKRIT TIRAVANIJA
A RETROSPECTIVE
(TOMORROW IS ANOTHER FINE DAY)

HET JAAR ROND MET BOL

Thomas Huber
SCHILDERKABINET

PAN PAN van George Belzer

MUSEUM BOIJMANS
VAN BEUNINGEN

MUSEUMPARK 18/20
NL-3015 CX ROTTERDAM
+31 10 441 9475

Peter Fischli
David Weiss

7 DEC '03
8 FEB '04

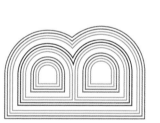

INFO@BOIJMANS.ROTTERDAM.NL
WWW.BOIJMANS.NL

BB-BOLD-1

abcdefghijklmnopq
rstuvwxyz

ABCDEFGHIJKLMNOPQ
RSTUVWXYZ

0123456789
@#$%^&*(){}+-=?!<>⟨⟩{}‚ "

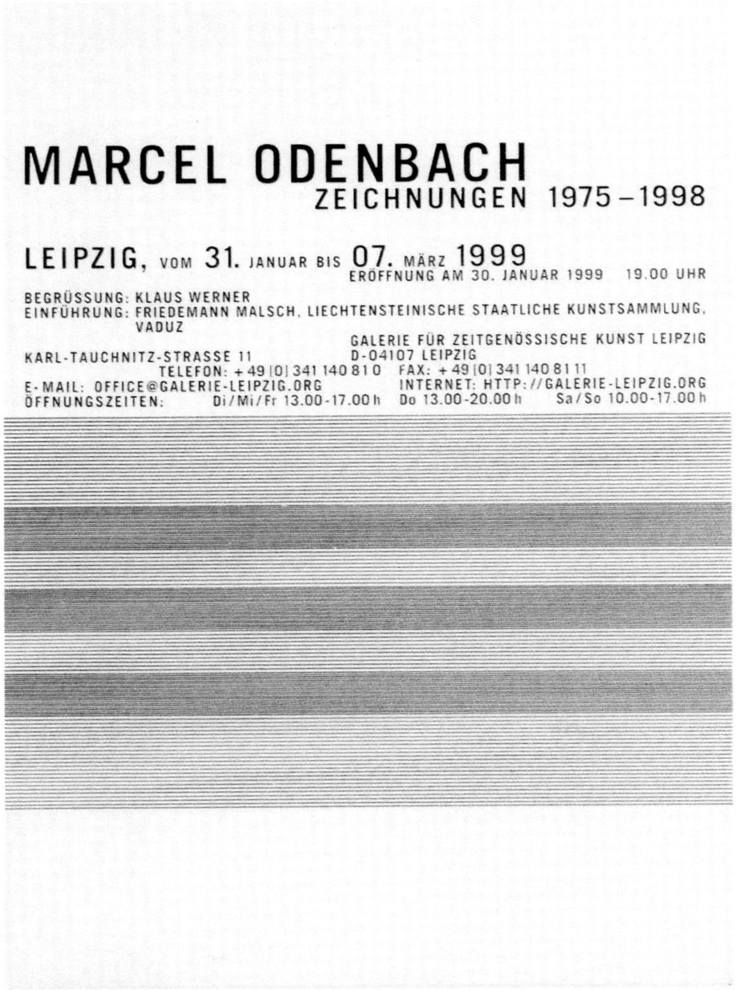

MARCEL ODENBACH

ZEICHNUNGEN 1975–1998

LEIPZIG, VOM 31. JANUAR BIS 07. MÄRZ 1999
ERÖFFNUNG AM 30. JANUAR 1999   19.00 UHR

BEGRÜSSUNG: KLAUS WERNER
EINFÜHRUNG: FRIEDEMANN MALSCH, LIECHTENSTEINISCHE STAATLICHE KUNSTSAMMLUNG,
VADUZ

GALERIE FÜR ZEITGENÖSSISCHE KUNST LEIPZIG
KARL-TAUCHNITZ-STRASSE 11
D-04107 LEIPZIG
TELEFON: +49(0)341 140 810   FAX: +49(0)341 140 811
E-MAIL: OFFICE@GALERIE-LEIPZIG.ORG   INTERNET: HTTP://GALERIE-LEIPZIG.ORG
ÖFFNUNGSZEITEN: Di/Mi/Fr 13.00–17.00h   Do 13.00–20.00h   Sa/So 10.00–17.00h

ÖFFENTLICH PRIVAT

PUBLICLY PRIVATE

DAS BILD DES PRIVATEN IN DER DEUTSCHEN NACHKRIEGSFOTOGRAFIE

06.09.03   Eröffnung/Opening

Leipzig, vom 07.09.03
           bis 09.11.03

Die Sammlung als Labor XVIII

Die Sammlung als Labor XIX

Eröffnung/Opening

Leipzig, vom 23.11.03
           bis 25.01.04

Galerie für Zeitgenössische Kunst Leipzig

Fabrice Hybert

TESTOO® MUSTER

LEIPZIG, VOM **19.** SEPTEMBER BIS **15.** OKTOBER **1997**

UNTERGRUNDMESSEHALLE, MARKTPLATZ LEIPZIG, MARKT 1 – GEÖFFNET: 13.00 BIS 18.00 UHR, MONTAGS GESCHLOSSEN

formationen: Galerie für Zeitgenössische Kunst Leipzig, Sternwartenstraße 4-6, 04103 Leipzig, Telefon: 0341/257 72 15, Fax: 0341/ 257 72 16, http://galerie-leipzig.de/testoo

efördert von: Alfried Krupp von Bohlen und Halbach-Stiftung, Association Française d'Action Artistique AFAA, Citroën Niederlassung Leipzig, Förderkreis der Leipziger Galerie für Zeitgenössische Kunst e.V., Institut Français de Leipzig, arow Leipzig Rail & Port AG, Kulturamt Leipzig, Kulturstiftung Sachsen, Leipziger Messe, Leipziger Messe Verlag, Lufthansa, Sachsen LB, Stadtwerke Leipzig, Videotronic International GmbH Rastatt, Wiemer & Trachte AG Leipzig

Galerie für zeitgenössische Kunst, Leipzig

(Case Study 10)

The Galerie für Zeitgenössische Kunst, Leipzig, founded in the 1990s, moved in 1998 into the "villa which was converted by Peter Kulka in the Nineties.... He followed the representative character of the architectural structure, reorganised them, kept the spatial arrangement and added unexpected views. Kulka's building followed inside the converted villa the concept of the white cube. He designed spaces, which allow a full concentration on art and its aesthetic qualities." [07] The Galerie is dedicated to "showing and increasing awareness of national and international artists.... Among the temporary exhibitions are annual collection presentations, there is a public library, lectures, workshops, book presentations, an education centre for children, young people and adults with its own exhibition space, a comprehensive stipendium programme and two prizes, one for artistic/graphic design and another for young artists from post-Communist countries. The Café and 'gfzk garten' have been and continue to be conceived and designed by artists." [08]

How can the changing programs, exhibitions, and events be moved to the foreground of the visual identity? By emphasizing the art and allowing all other elements to be put at its service; i.e., being flexible enough to adapt to changing contents. In contrast to many visual identities, the name of the gallery recedes into the background; instead, the very nature of "contemporary art in Leipzig" is quite literally the theme: "Hic et nunc"—"here and now"—"at this place and at this time" is written on the façade of the building. A linear structure visualizing the metaphor of collecting serves as an additional element: individual branches are brought together into a bundle. At the same time, the structure works as a transition, as a connecting element or graphic texture: "Like a filter placed between the observer and the depicted object. This filter is the gallery." [09] The linear structure

[07] Galerie für zeitgenössische Kunst, Leipzig, www.gfzk-online.de/de/index.php?menue=27&pos=8.
[08] Galerie für Zeitgenössische Kunst, Leipzig, www.gfzk-online.de/de/index.php?menue=29&pos=1.
[09] Markus Dreßen, personal interview, 2006.

can simultaneously be read as a reference to media, reminiscent of the linear structure of a video image. While date and location form the constants on the level of the signified, aspects of the signifier can vary; e. g., in typography or color. In contrast to the two aforementioned visual identities, constant and variable are in direct relationship across the shared level of the signified. "The content constant allows the formal design to be handled relatively freely. It enables a statement to be made about the content that is specific to the situation. The poster for Fabrice Hybert [fig. 1, pp. 94–95], for example, shows a film. The characteristic of film, the movement of the images, is translated into the style of the linear structure: the pictures run from top to bottom and the structure in between brings to mind interference, the flickering of a video." [10]

Fully developed, flexible visual identities can generate situation-specific variations — as highlighted here — because they create constancy and coherence via an open, basically formulated rule. Since only the signified side of the sign is stipulated by the rule, the specific theme of the implementation can be varied in design on the signifier side.

Visual identity by students of the Hochschule für Grafik und Buchkunst, Leipzig: Markus Dreßen, Gabriele Altevers, Birgit Piramovsky, and Kerstin Riedel; with Günter Karl Bose and Ruedi Baur (project direction). In use from autumn 1996 to spring 2000.

[10] Ibid.

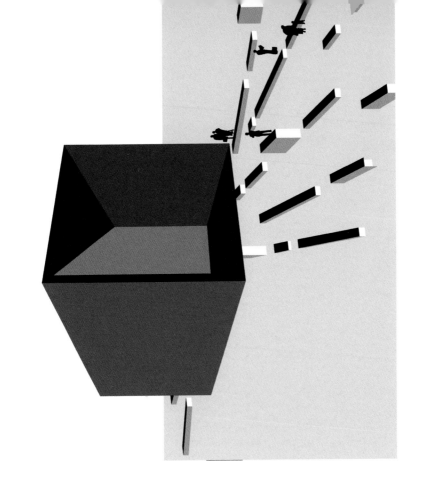

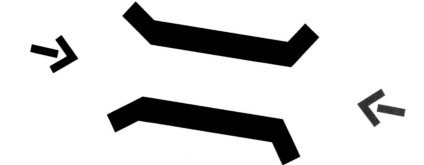

Museion – Museum für moderne und zeitgenössische Kunst, Bozen

(Case Study 11)

Self-Similarity

Laws of self-similarity are found in nature in, for example, trees, the circulatory system, river systems, and coastlines. The principle of self-similarity means that forms that are similar to each other appear on various scales or in different size relationships. A distinction can be made between strict self-similarity, as with ferns and Romanesco broccoli (a variety of cauliflower), and loose self-similarity, such as between lime trees and their leaves. Self-similarity may not only be seen in nature at spatial distances but also in the

The Museion – Museum für moderne und zeitgenössische Kunst, Bozen, opened its newly constructed building in spring 2008. It describes itself as an "open museum": "The building's cubic shape is charged with strong visual impact, and the architecture itself is a vehicle of dialogue: the front and rear façades are largely transparent, and place the city's historical centre in dialogue with some of its more recent areas, as well as with the meadows that flank the Talvera River. The new Museion building presents itself as an equally physical and symbolic links (sic) between the two parts of the city.... The building's interior spaces are highly fluid: the various levels of museum activity — exhibition and per-formance areas, didactic workshops, library, cafeteria and shop— are not rigidly separated from one another, but are intimately interconnected." [11] The special feature of Museion, Bozen thus primarily lies in its architecture. When read like a sign, the main characteristic is its "passage-like nature": it is divided into two long closed sides and two short open fronts, a shape taking up the spatial experience of a modern-day tunnel crossing of the Alps, with the rapid, drastic change of cultural and landscape spaces. The museum space positions itself in a direct rather than merely symbolic relationship to the Brenner Pass transit area, one of the most important connections between Austria and Italy.

The visual identity begins with this characteristic and connects it with the semantic field of the concept of "passage," including both "transit" and "journey" as well as "passing" ("happening," "going past," "going through"), [12] a change in which both a spatial as well as a chronological connotation appears. Concrete images connect with the semantic field: the image of the street, the road, the canal, or the bridge — the track of a directional movement. The elementary design principle emerges from these various concepts, situated in a specific spatial arrangement of

[11] Museion – Museum für moderne und zeitgenössische Kunst, Bozen, www.museion.it/ #das_neue_museion&0&en. [12] See Kluge, Etymologisches Wörterbuch der deutschen Sprache, p. 615.

99

MUSEUM FOR MUSEION
MUSEUM FÜR MODERNE UND ZEITGENÖSSISCHE KUNST BOZEN
MUSEION
MODERN AND CONTEMPORARY ART

MUSEUM FOR MODERN AND CONTEMPORARY ART MUSEION

FABRICE HYBERT
OBJETS 12 / 06 / 08

MUSEUM FÜR MODERNE UND ZEITGENÖSSISCHE KUNST

BOLZANO / BOZEN

MUSEO D'ARTE MODERNA E CONTEMPORANEA

the elements: two long sides through which something moves. This arrangement alludes not only to the architecture and the changing exhibitions, but to exhibition visitors as well.

The visual identity is essentially based on the fact that this principle is depicted in all the permutations: a potential change in dimension entails a change in the degree of abstraction. The basic logo displays the most reduced, pictogram-like form of this principle: the cartographic sign for a mountain pass. [Fig. 1, p. 98] Realized typographically, signs, type, and images move through two bars. [Fig. 4, p. 100] In three-dimensional space, elements of signage take over the "movement through the passage." Here it becomes particularly clear: the signage begins on the walls inside and continues outside on cube-shaped seating elements. Their arrangement visualizes movement through the building. [Fig. 2, p. 98; fig. 2, p. 100]

Visual identity by Intégral Ruedi Baur and Denis Coueignoux (laboratoire irb).

This design is an unrealized competition submission. Year of origin: 2007

dimension of time. The shapes of the oscillation of a drop of water show self-similar structures to the shell of an adult tortoise. [Fig. 1, p. 78] The process of the variation of a design principle described is close to the principle of self-similarity: forms similar to each other are seen on various scales or in different size relationships.

Figs. 1–2, p. 99: There is more, free self-similarity between a lime tree leaf and a lime tree.

Fig. 1, p. 101: Brenner Pass (project reference)

Variation through Changing Degrees of Abstraction

In everyday life we are frequently confronted with different formal representations of the same thing. In the field of geographical cartography, for example, maps serve various functions and therefore employ various levels of abstraction. And increasingly they appear in parallel with Internet presentations, where users can easily choose between various forms to suit their specific purpose. As the choice of potential image samples in the representation of different degrees of abstraction is rather large, it is essential for a visual identity that this variety does not jeopardize its inner coherence.

From top left: **Fig. 1, p. 102**: Drawing; **fig. 2, p. 102**: Architectural model; **fig. 3, p. 102**: Aerial photograph; **fig. 4, p. 102**: Google Maps, Map view; **fig. 5, p. 102**: Google Maps, Terrain view; **fig. 6, p. 102**: Google Maps, Satellite view; **fig. 1, p. 103**: Photography; **fig. 2, p. 103**: Historical map

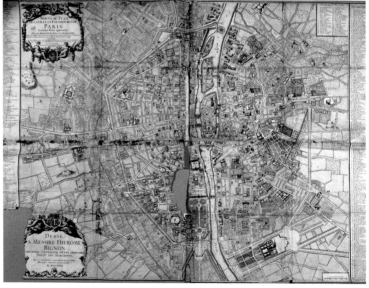

Ferropolis

(Case Study 12)

In 1995, staff from Bauhaus Dessau founded Ferropolis on the site of the Golpa-Nord strip mine in Sachsen-Anhalt. "Ferropolis is intended to be a museum, an art object, a venue for meetings and events, a café, a stage, a research and development station, and a youth hostel…. It is an attempt at the visualization of an industrial garden realm at a specific location and is also intended to function as an object of identification and impulse outside the region. A configuration of huge mining machines creates a sculpture that the public can walk around and is at the same time a striking landmark — the 'City of Iron.'… The project has a decisive role for the future of people in this region since it can become a means of livelihood and also a motivation for new pathways and projects…. Processes determine our life. All of life is an overlapping of processes. They run at various speeds, many over such long time periods that we are not aware of them. Many processes are not visible to us. Many processes have a not-inconsiderable effect on us. We trigger many processes. A construction site makes changes visible in a relatively short time span. A construction site is a world in miniature. A cauliflower floret or only a part of a part of a cauliflower floret. Ferropolis is a construction site. Stone for stone, moment for moment, something is created, something can disappear or be dug up again. The process is too complicated and multi-layered for our perception. We visualize the process in a series of pictures and stages. Moments remain for us in memory." [13]

The visual identity is based on the visualization of processes. On the levels of form and content the interrelationship between individual and group, part and whole, and general and specific is taken as a theme. A zoom movement serves as a visual analogy that is visualized through the frames and appropriate details. The frame indicates the respective observation scale like a navi-

Images, Concepts and Understanding

"Clouds are not spheres, mountains are not cones, coastlines are not circles…. The number of distinct scales of length of natural patterns is for all practical purposes infinitive. The existence of these patterns challenges us to study those forms that Euclid leaves aside as being 'formless,' to investigate the morphology of the 'amorphous.'… Scientists will (I am sure) be surprised and delighted to find that not a few shapes they had to call grainy, hydralike, in between, pimply, pocky, seaweedy, strange, tangled, tortuous, wiggly, wispy, wrinkled, and the like, can henceforth be approached in rigorous and vigorous quantitative fashion." [14]

Fractal geometry not only provides scientists with new observation criteria, but also other concepts with which to describe their observations and thus communicate them. Inversely, through visualization a visual identity makes phenomena comprehensible.

[13] Antje Reineck, unpublished manuscript, n. pag. [14] Benoit Mandelbrot, The Fractal Geometry of Nature, pp. 1–5; cited in: The ABC's of Triangle Square Circle, p. 60.

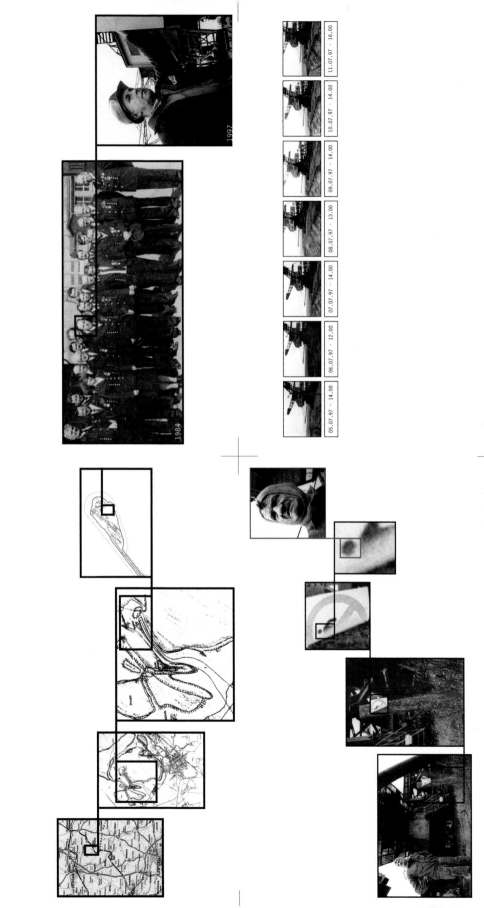

05.07.97 - 14.00 06.07.97 - 12.00 07.07.97 - 14.00 08.07.97 - 13.00 09.07.97 - 14.00 10.07.97 - 14.00 11.07.97 - 16.00

1984

1997

gator. "Frames convey the content. Frame references depict the zoom movement; time bars and time and date information make up the chronological classification. Contrasts and sequences of frames create connections and show dimensions. Optically the structure concentrates the project as an entity but is nevertheless so variable that the processual is integrated. A fixed sign cannot stand for a process. In contrast, the graphic structure becomes a medium for continually updated information." [15]

Visual identity by Antje Reineck. Diploma project realized at the Hochschule für Grafik und Buchkunst, Leipzig. Year of origin: 1997

    [15] Antje Reineck, unpublished manuscript, n. pag.

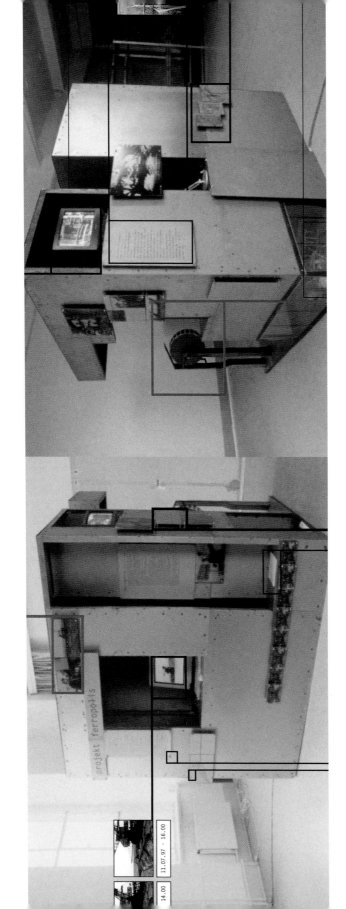

projekt ferropolis

11.07.97 - 16.00

14.00

Self-similarity

Fig. 1, p. 108: "The flower of a wild carrot with its characteristic spiral structure, a structure that can also be found in sunflower seeds, pine cones, pineapples, etc." [16]

Figs. 1–2, p. 109: "The spiral arrangement of the seeds of the pine cone [fig. 1] and individual small blossoms of the sunflower [fig. 2] are based on the principle of the 'golden ratio.' [Fig. 3, p. 109:] 'Standing wave,' 52.4 Hertz." [17]

Figs. 4–6, p. 109: "The typical pattern of two spirals in opposite directions (in a pine cone 1 to the left and 8 to the right) can only be achieved in computer reconstruction with precise adherence to the 'golden angle' at 137.5 degrees [fig. 5], at 136.5 degrees [fig. 4], and at 138 degrees [fig. 6]." [18]

[16] Paolo Portoghesi, Nature and Architecture, p. 86.   [17] Alexander Lauterwasser, Wasser Klang Bilder, p. 101.   [18] Ibid.

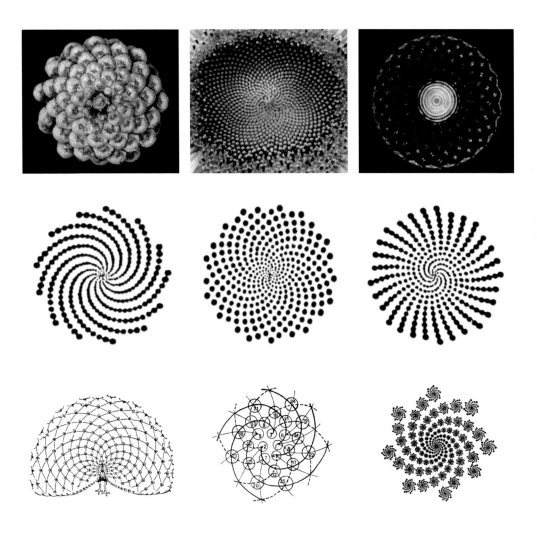

Cinémathèque française

(Case Study 07, Part 2)

A description of the Cinémathèque française can be found in chapter 2.

The first step towards simplification and generalization is through
the use of a synecdoche, a figure of speech by which a term representing either a more specific or more general class is used to
refer to another term (e. g. keel for ship) — here, "(projected)
light" is the synecdoche for "cinema." One type of synecdoche
is pars pro toto, as in the example, "we all live under one roof,"
also known as metonymy.

Light is projected in the form of a rectangular projection plane
with blurred edges, thus simulating an actual projection, appearing as white or colored planes and forms that represent variable
perspectives. This form of variation in perspective is discussed
in detail in chapter 2.

The visual identity is based on a constant signifier — the projection
plane — in its variable depictions across different media. In two-
dimensional realizations, such as in print or on the Internet, the
projection is simulated, i. e. graphically represented, and is often
accompanied by other elements that appear projected, for example, the typeface, a reworking of Alpha Headline in which the
rounded ends of the lines and corners give the letters a "blurred"
look. The principle of projection is also taken up in connection
with film stills: the stills themselves are not shown, but rather projected representations of the cinematic images. When the projected image is a continual film sequence, the actual projection
is also animated, i.e., in motion.

Within the three-dimensional spaces — such as the lobby, the
exhibition spaces, and the Cinémathèque library — light is used
directly, i. e. as real projections, thus facilitating the physical
experiencing of the space that is implied by the perspective of
the signs: text is printed on the wall and illuminated by the "projection plane." Objects moving in front of the signage will cast a

shadow. Space is not volume, as might be assumed with a "spatial sign," but rather a spatial quality is integrated representationally into the visual identity. In addition, the progression of typographic logos indicates the orientation of the spaces, thus leading visitors through the complex, convoluted system of rooms. Fixed-installation projectors execute the projections, and the entire visual staging within the lobby is changed twice a year. Thus, the cost of the visual identity is rather high at the beginning, but because "manual" signage — normally produced, for example, with various cutting plotters — is not needed, the costs in comparison to other organizations are relatively low.

Visual identity by Ruedi Baur, Olivier Duzelier, Toan Vu-Huu, Stéphanie Brabant (project coordination), Intégral Ruedi Baur et associés, Paris; Cinematic projections: Thomas Hundt, Ingo Zirngibl (creative direction), Oliver Fuchs (project management), Marcel Michalski, and Jörg Stierle (animation design) (www.janglednerves.com). Project period: 2004–2006

EXPOSITION PERMANENTE

CINEMAS

EXPOSITION TEMPORAIRE

MEDIATHÈQUE   ATELIERS

SALLE GEORGES FRANJU

QUARTIER
DES SPECTACLES
RUE SAINTE-CATHERINE | MONTRÉAL

EXCENTRIS
CHAPELLE DU BON PASTEUR
CÉGEP THÉÂTRE
ST-DENIS
CABARET
MUSÉE
CINÉMATHÈQUE QUÉBÉCOISE
BIBLIOTHÈQUE NATIONALE
COEUR
SALLE DES SCIENCES
JUSTE POUR RIRE
ÉGLISE WILFRID PELLETIER CINÉMATHÈQUE QUÉBÉCOISE
ST-JAMES MUSÉE MÉTROPOLIS BIBLIOTHÈQUE NATIONALE
CINÉMA D'ART CONTEMPORAIN CENTRE DU QUÉBEC
IMPÉRIAL MAISONNEUVE PLACE DES ARTS FOUFOUNES PIERRE-PELADEAU
MAISONNEUVE ÉLECTRIQUES

SPECTRUM COMPLEXES CLUB SODA UQAM
BELGO DES JARDINS MONUMENT NATIONAL
GÉSU CINÉMA THÉÂTRE SAT MÉDLEY
PARISIEN DU NOUVEAU MONDE

PALAIS
DES CONGRÈS

QUARTIER
DES SPECTACLES
RUE SAINTE-CATHERINE | MONTRÉAL

Quartier des spectacles

(Case Study 13)

Stagings in Public Space

In each concrete stage-managed composition there is not only mediation between the design of the stage, its objects, and the actors and costumes, but also between their movements, entrances, and exits. By a designer of public space, these components can only be imagined up to a certain point. Nevertheless, the atmosphere of a place depends to a great extent upon the degree of sensitivity with which the levels are attuned. Stagings in public space require a high level of flexibility, because the passers-by entering the "scene" change continually. But it is not only the people that change, but also their perspective, which can be that of an "actor," that of an audience member watching an actor, or someone completely uninvolved in the scene. In a scene witnessed by others, still another scene, another perspective, is generated, that which is from the exterior, from outside the scene. The design must therefore be open enough for the widest range of scenes: it should neither compete with the people nor remain completely detached.

The Quartier des spectacles, Montréal, does not define itself through administrative boundaries but with its thirty-five distinct cultural venues grouped around Rue Sainte-Catherine. Together they form one of the cultural centers of Montreal, even though it is at present characterized by prostitution and drug dealing and thus a less attractive area to live and work. A new visual identity is to serve as an engine to improve the district's public image. One of the principal aims is to give the thirty-five distinct buildings an overall identity without detracting from their individuality. The superordinate visual identity should represent very different types of events and appeal to a wide public.

For this visual identity, light also specifies the signified, not in the sense of "projection" but of "illumination." The constant figure is a red circular area that simulates "lighting" with its blurred edges, evoking an element of a LED display. The principle of lighting forms another constant that is transferred to all main elements, such as the typography and the various textures on venue façades. In the basic logo, the circular area is extended into a line of circles representing the main axis of the district, Rue Sainte-Catherine. [Figs. 1–4, p. 114] In addition, the basic logo is formed from text blocks and an abstraction of a city map of the quarter. In the various derivations of the basic logo, the city plan contains areas that vary in representation from clear articulation to dissolution.

As with the visual identity of the Cinémathèque française, simulated and real physical lighting alternate in accordance with the communication media used. Two facets of light are thus conveyed. As a graphic sign it is a symbolic light, evoking Broadway, the stage, and the world of appearance and illusion, alluding to the act of revealing and concealing on stage. On the façade, the lighting is real: at each venue, the illuminated spot clearly dis-

"In my work I often don't put the loud-speakers at head height so that the sounds I use don't compete with what the people are saying or with what they naturally hear from the walls. It's similarly resolved in the Quartier des spectacles: the lights give the space its depth with regard to people passing by. The projections on the ground and the façade envelop passers-by; they are accompanied by the traces of light rather than dominated by them. In contrast to a shopping center that is brightly lit twenty-four hours a day in order to keep shoppers and employees awake, the red light here creates a mysterious atmosphere extending an invitation to passers-by." [19]

plays whether it is open for the public. Venues illuminated together indicate specific cycles and groupings of events. This aspect will be dealt with in more detail in chapter IV.

Visual identity by Ruedi Baur, Antje Kolm, and Axel Steinberger, Intégral Ruedi Baur, Zurich; and Jean Beaudoin, Intégral Jean Beaudoin Montréal (www.integral.jeanbeaudoin.com). Project period: since 2005

Beaux-arts de Paris

(Case Study 14)

The École nationale supérieure des beaux-arts de Paris (ENSBA),
known as Beaux-arts de Paris, is a French public art academy
where, in a five-year course, the foundations of the artistic process are taught in connection with contemporary art production.
The university is divided into three departments with the empha-
sis on artistic practice, theory of art, and technical training. In
addition to permanent lecturers, regularly invited artists enhance
the curriculum. [20]

The constant of the visual identity is derived from the traces of
tools used at an art school, currently characterized by the complementary relationship of "manual" versus "digital." As the
difference between the traces left by brush, pencil, and computer
would be too great, the range of tools was limited to graphic
textures.
The two fundamentally different tool types produce a group of
textures that leave different impressions. Computer-generated
textures are rather systematic: horizontal, vertical, and diagonal
connections within a grid. [Fig. 1, p. 122 and fig. 1, p. 124] In contrast,
hand-drawn curves are dominated by free movement and the
flow of the hand. [Fig. 3, p. 122 and fig. 2, p. 124] Both types are used
both in positive and negative. Texture densities indicate textual
hierarchies; the posters, for example, feature three distinct densities. The textures overlay the lettering and image levels, creating a painting-like impression.
All other means are very simple and reduced: only basic colors
are used, mainly the complementary colors red and green. The
system font Verdana, designed for optimal screen display for
Microsoft by Matthew Carter in 1996, stands out for its generous
proportions and spacing between letters. The Verdana Bold
re-worked for the Beaux-arts de Paris is rather well suited to be
superimposed with textures. The simple, reduced means

[20] See École nationale supérieure des beaux-arts de Paris,
www.ensba.fr/informations/informationsEnglish.htm.

employed in the visual identity create a strong contrast to the fine lines of the textures.

Visual identity by Ruedi Baur, Stéphanie Brabant, and Olivier Duzelier, Intégral Ruedi Baur et associés, Paris; and Denis Coueignoux (laboratoire irb).
Project period: 2006–2008

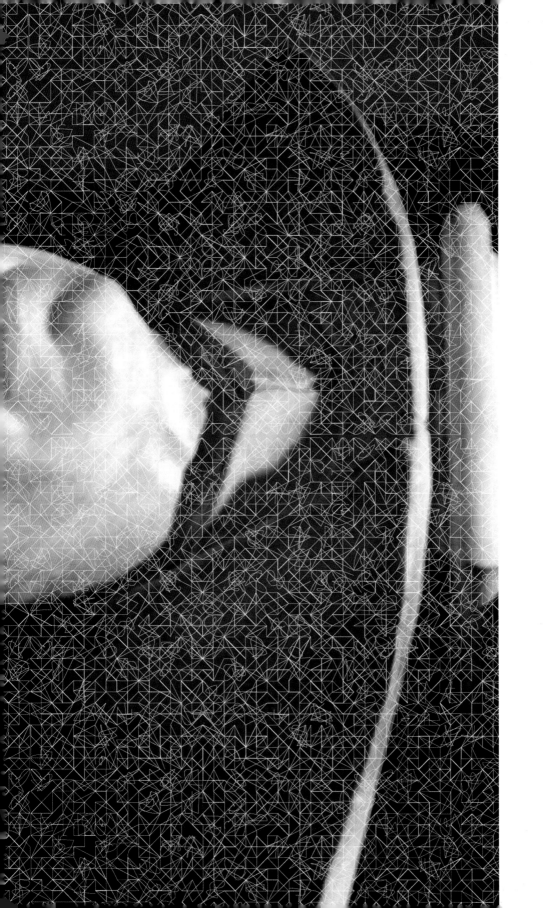

Beaux-arts
de Paris
l'école nationale
supérieure
Livret
de l'étudiant
2007-2008

ministère de la culture et de la communication

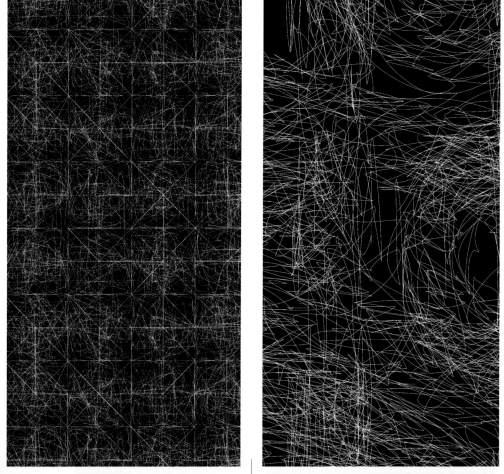

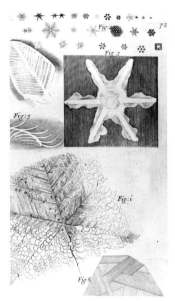

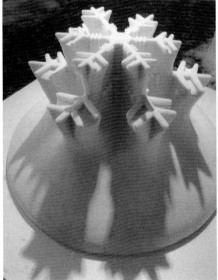

Variation through Change in the Form of Representation

"The snowflake is the beauty queen of the Solid State. She reveals herself in an abundance of different shapes and appearances. She is cited for her fickleness as well as for her constancy, for although she never appears twice in exactly the same configuration, her symmetry is invariably hexagonal; when any snowflake is turned 60° around an axis perpendicular to its plane, its original appearance is reproduced." [21]

Within the diversity of means and forms of representation that produces the infinite variety of the snowflake — simultaneously evoking different contextual connotations — lies vast design potential for the development of visual identities.

Fig. 1, p. 123: Illustrated in drawing: "Images of snowflakes showing six-sided symmetry and ice crystals." [22]
Fig. 2, p. 123: Illustrated in a sculpture by Japanese artist Yutaka Sone, entitled "(large) marble snowflake."

Fig. 3, p. 123: Illustrated in a scan from a scanning electron microscope: "Ordinary hexagonal dendrite snowflake, highly magnified by a low-temperature scanning electron microscope." [23]

[21] Arthur L. Loeb, The Architecture of Crystals, p. 38.   [22] NOAA Photo Library, www.photolib.noaa.gov/htmls/libroo66.htm.   [23] http://commons.wikimedia.org/wiki/Image:Snow_crystals_2b.png.

Beaux-arts
de Paris
l'école nationale
supérieure

Livret
de l'étudiant
2007–2008

Portes
Ouvertes des
Beaux-arts de
Paris l'école
nationale
supérieure

Vendredi 29 juin 2007 de 11h à 23h / Samedi 30 juin
2007 de 11h à 20h / Visites des ateliers, expositions
«Cadrage→Débordement» et «Ardoises, petits papiers
&...», concerts, performances, lectures, installations,
projections, etc. / 14, rue Bonaparte 75006 Paris /
13, quai Malaquais 75006 Paris / tél 01 47 03 50 73
www.beauxartsparis.fr

Buvette LINAS

ministère de la Culture et de la Communication

Portes
Ouvertes
des Beaux-
arts de
Paris l'école
nationale
supérieure

Visites des ateliers, expositions
«Cadrage Débordement» et «Ardoises,
Petits papiers &...», concerts, performances,
lectures, installations, projection, etc...
Vendredi 29 juin 2007 de 11h à 23h
samedi 30 juin 2007 de 11h à 20h - 14, rue
Bonaparte 75006 Paris - tél 01 47 03 50 73
www.beauxartsparis.fr

Summary

The first examples cited in this chapter illustrate the transition of a singular logo into a flexible visual identity, specifically the logo variations of the International Red Cross and Red Crescent Movement and Dutch PTT. Self-contained signs, logo-like and modified in shape and color, appear independently, but are nevertheless connected by common attributes. While logo variations can certainly represent a spectrum of activities, they are less effective than flexible visual identities at simultaneously representing the stable core of an organization and its variable fields of activity. For this it needs the interaction between a basic logo and sign family formed by variation processes.

In some cases, a special relationship crystallizes: the individual parts form a correlation with an overarching (meta-)visual identity and sub-visual identities. Such is the case, for example, with the Frankfurter Kunstverein, where independent sub-visual identities are developed typographically. This pyramiding can be implemented more or less systematically. In the visual identity of the Frankfurter Kunstverein there is no explicit visual constant, instead continuous discernibility is surrendered in favor of a visual identity that "permanently reinvents itself." And yet, coherence is stylistically created on a visual level, for example, through the use of montage, and, of course, the institution's name, "Frankfurter Kunstverein," appears in every permutation.

Constants and variations can appear in visual identities as separate elements or combined in a sign, which in the case of the Frankfurter Kunstverein is constructed from both the constant and variable aspects. In the visual identity of the Museum Boijmans van Beuningen Rotterdam, the self-contained typographical level, "Boijman's font," forms the constant. Here there is no directly visible interplay between constant and variable. For the visual identity of the Galerie für zeitgenössische Kunst, Leipzig, the date and location — a constant signified — is pre-

Summary

sented alongside a signifier with variable features, principally
the font, but also color and size. With a linear structure serving
as an additional constant element, constant and variable are
thus combined in a sign.

When a visual identity is based not on constant elements but
rather on a constant principle, as with the Museion, Bozen and
its visual identity based upon the "passage-like," the constant
shifts more deeply into the structure of the sign family. The constant is now no longer a property of an individual sign — a certain form, color, or materiality — but more a principle characteristic. In this example, it is in a specific spatial configuration:
there are always two long, closed sides through which something moves. What the two sides are composed of — be it two bars
or two walls — and what moves through them is variable. The
constant principle is not limited to being represented in various
degrees of abstraction, but allows each implementation — basic
logo, typographical use, three-dimensional space — to reproduce
the significant principle of the visual identity in its own media-
specific way. Thus, the variations become more specific and the
dynamics collectively increase.

The visual identities of the Cinémathèque française and the
Quartier des spectacles function in a similar way: they use an elemental signifier — "light" — deployed across all media. In the
former, the greatest difference arises between two-dimensional
graphic representation and three-dimensional real projection.
As a sign, "light" is very general and abstract, while at the same
time being incredibly specific. The fact that signified and signifier coincide is particularly unusual as the sign appears directly
as what it represents — as "light." Thus, as discussed in chapter
IV, another facet more clearly emerges: the direct, the instanta-
neous, and event-like character as experienced at a performance.
The visual identity of the Beaux-arts de Paris is based on the

Summary

constant use of various texture-like traces of tools, which conveys above all the interplay between manual and digital techniques.

04.
Combinatorics: Rapports / Modules / Elementary Construction Kits

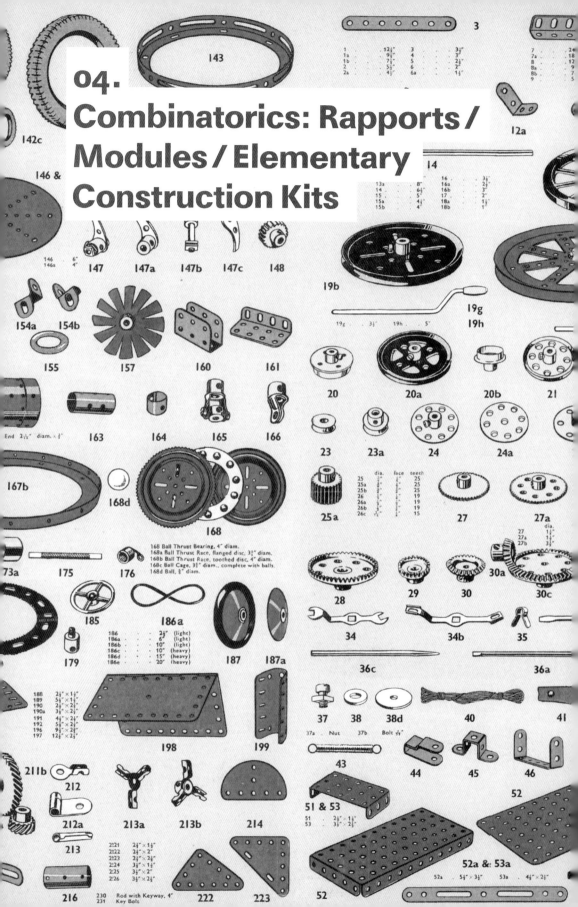

In order to elucidate the difference between this chapter and the one that precedes it, we preface the following with a quote from Richard Paul Lohse as its motto: "Increasingly, the additive principal transformed itself into an ordering system of relationships, the sequence into reciprocal mobility." [01]

A rapport (pattern repeat) is among the simple systems with which elements are repeated and mirrored, illustrated here with the example of the visual identity of Aktau Marina Residential District, Kazakhstan. The properties of modularity will then be illustrated with two examples: the detergent packaging of Teddy-mat, Teddy 75, and Roby 75; and a poster series for Oper Leipzig. The main part of the chapter is taken up with three very different visual identities, on the basis of which one can see the beginnings of a trend towards systematization: the visual identity for ABM Warenhauskette, based on a modular construction system of elementary forms; the visual identity for Rotterdam 2001, Culture Capital of Europe, in which elementary geometrical figures are dissolved and combined with each other in varying proportions; and the visual identity for SSH Utrecht, a social housing organization. This case study takes up a special place in the chapter insofar as reciprocal relationships are constructed principally on the level of color. By means of the interplay of constant and variable, the theme explored here is the relationship between individual and collective, general and specific.

Fig. 1, p. 128: Meccano construction
kit parts

[01] Richard Paul Lohse, in: Lohse lesen, p. 215.

Aktau Marina Residential District, Kazakhstan

(Case Study 15)

The Kazakh city of Aktau (formerly Shevchenko in Russian) lies in the west of Kazakhstan on the Caspian Sea. As with many former Soviet cities, the architecture of Aktau is characterized by great standardization and an egalitarian urban structure. "From the very beginning the structure of the 'plan city' (sic) Shevchenko was based upon typical concepts of Soviet urban planning. A strict separation of functions as well as the foundation of dense microdistricts were of big importance. Thus a clear edge between city and steppe areas became characteristic." [02]

Creating characteristic differences in the uniform cityscape represents a considerable challenge, particularly as the decades-long dominance of socialism in public space produced the almost complete disappearance of Kazakh folk culture. Surprisingly, however, these days the traditional yurt has been revived as a powerful symbol of Kazakh tradition: the Kazakh coat of arms has the crown of a yurt at its center. The visual identity takes up this connection and attempts to reintegrate the wealth of an almost invisible tradition back into the cityscape. Traditional yurts were richly decorated with tapestries and colorful embroidery, the patterns and geometrical motifs of which provide the inspiration for the development of contemporary grids and patterns.

The visual identity is based on the constant use of continually modified patterns, the areas of which are enclosed by frames reminiscent of carpet braiding. The patterns are adapted to specific situations and can change in parallel to the development of the city. Russian is still the predominant language in Kazakhstan, though the role of Kazakh as the official national language has grown steadily since the declaration of independence in 1991. Using the Fedra Multiscript font, developed by Peter Bilak with Russian and Roman character sets, enables bilingual realization. The color spectrum is defined by the material of the respective

Figs. 1–2, p. 130: The specific local context is reflected in the visual identity. The historical carpet patterns of the nomads thus form the basis for the patterns that appear, for example, in parking lots (project reference).

Figs. 1–3, p. 133: Mosaics and patterns of baroque gardens (project reference)

[02] Shevchenko/Aktau: The Heritage of an Ideal Socialist City, www.kasachstanprojekt.de/pdfdownload/microdistricts_and_the_city_centre.pdf.

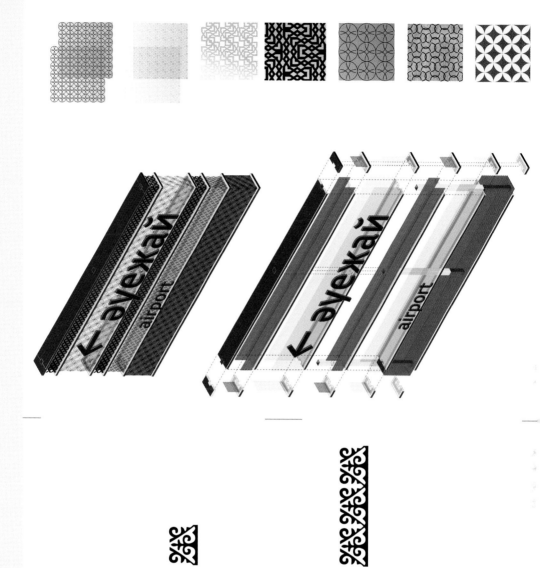

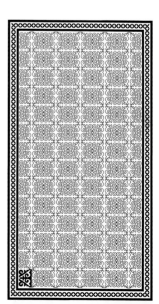

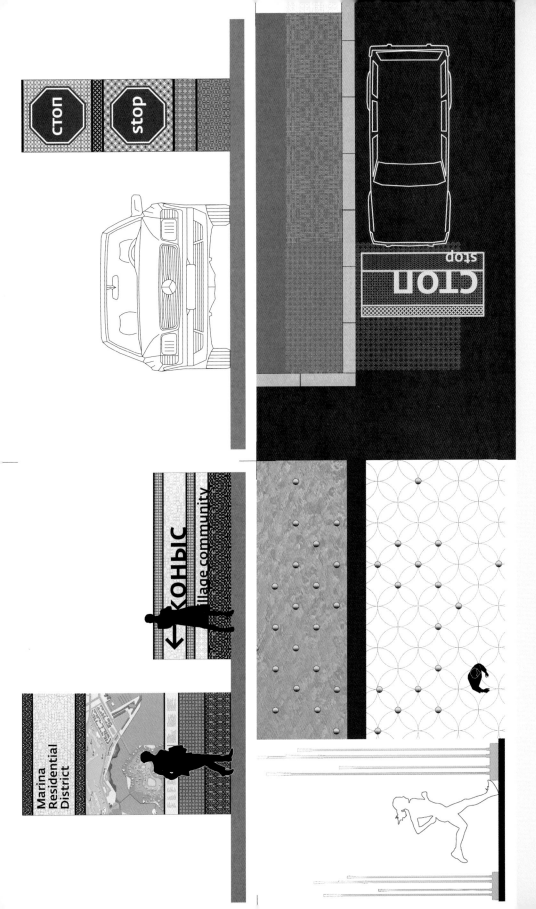

object: steel (gray and silver), concrete (light gray and beige), or glass. Glass and concrete thus appear imprinted with color. The patterns can appear as textile, wall and façade decoration, as floor mosaics, and as lawn and hedge mazes. In many variations, such as on information panels, they function as a decorative element. In contrast, however, on streets and in parking lots they also cause a shift of one's perception of reality; the decorative braiding of a carpet pattern transforms the coarse asphalt into a "fine parlor." The "carpeting" of the streets makes the outdoors seem indoors. [Fig. 3, p. 132] The layering of several carpets evokes magnificent palace halls, and the black and white representation of the patterns in the graphic versions champions the contemporary style of carpets. As determined carpet patterns are traditionally associated with certain families or clans, the visual identity has the potential to establish specific relationships and develop a cultural topology. In the illumination of the harbor promenade, the pattern establishes the arrangement of the light poles, thus providing an inner structure. In the permutations of this project can be seen a wide spectrum of variability, ranging from visible ornament to invisible inner structure. [Fig. 4, p. 132]

Visual identity by Ruedi Baur (artistic direction), Simon Burkart, Christiane Hoegner (industrial design), Eva Kubinyi (coordination, graphic design direction), Wanja Ledowski (graphic design direction) and Mathieu Meyer (graphic design), Intégral Ruedi Baur et associés, Paris. Year of origin: 2007

Fundação
Champalimaud

Champalimaud Foundation

Rapport / Pattern / Visual Echoes

The German dictionary of foreign words defines "rapport" (Fr.) as "the repetition of patterns or motifs." [03] To this we might add, "rapport can be applied not only to motifs but also to colors, materials, materialities, and motif structures." [04] Within a pattern, the smallest self-contained individual element is called the "rapport." When the "rapport" is repeated — "repeat" (Fr.: rapport) — it forms the pattern. The rapport forms the constant while, for example, its orientation or its dimensions can change. In the visual identity of the city of Aktau, the contemporary modification distinguishes itself from traditional patterns principally by the fact that the rapport element is small and recedes into the background, thus the sense of texture, rather than that of the individual ornament, dominates.
[Fig. 1, p. 131]

The Champalimaud Foundation is a private organization supporting research projects in the field of medical science. Its visual identity is based on the constant initials, "CF," the letter forms of which develop out of a circle. In some variations, such as the back of foundation stationary or on wrapping paper, the initials are arranged into distinct patterns. The variations in the visual appearance result from different proportions within the rapport. Depending on the size, the individual motif remains dominant [see the 4th page in the sequence in fig. 1, p. 134] or recedes into the background in favor of the overall effect of the pattern. [See the 1st page in the sequence in fig. 1, p. 134]
Diversity is also produced through different forms of overprinting, zoom, and layout, and through the varied exploitation of the dynamics of the circular form.

Visual identity by Studio Dumbar. Project period: since 2005

[03] Duden, Das Fremdwörterbuch, p. 661.   [04] Judith Hess, personal interview, 2008.

Cut-ups

Each poster in this series is itself a modular system of poster elements. Once printed, a poster can be hung as it is, or cut up and reassembled in a manner appropriate to a specific location. As the parts remain moveable until the composition is fixed, both a collage and its possible variations are inherent in the original poster, on which the trim and registration marks are particularly suggestive. And yet, they do not only specify the possible layout positions, but also characterize the temporary, dynamic expression of the series that is present even when the montage is not effected.

Poster series by Markus Dreßen and Kerstin Riedel, with Günter-Karl Bose (project direction). Year of origin: 1997

Figs. 1-2, p. 136: Poster for "Die Nase" (an opera by Dmitri Shostakovich), from the poster series for Oper Leipzig.

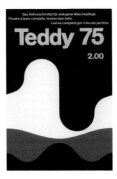

Teddymat, Teddy 75, and Roby 75

The nature of modularity is exhibited in the detergent packaging of Teddymat, Teddy 75, and Roby 75. The three variants produce a series, but also, "The waves form a continuous pattern over the different packs. This occurs irre- spective of whether the packs standing side by side are identical or different. It also occurs when the ends and faces of packs are placed side by side." [05] Each surface can be combined with every other. Each "wave" part, by itself and with reference to the whole, conveys the stylized movement of water. The shared points of intersection — the "plugs" that enable Lego bricks to connect — are the basis of this modularity.

Visual identity by Karl Gerstner (www.karlgerstner.de). Year of origin: 1964

Figs. 1-2, p. 137: Teddymat, Teddy 75, and Roby 75

[05] Karl Gerstner, Designing Programmes, p. 16.

ABM Warenhauskette

(Case Study 16)

Concrete Poetry

"The additive principal transformed itself more and more into an ordering system of relationships, the sequence into reciprocal mobility. The analogy to problems of constructive art, especially with the development of serial orders, becomes recognizable. The individual element is standardized and developed into a controllable and measurable quantity with the aim of creating a structural identity between the visual means and the limit of the image, and the aim of creating objective rhythmics. The standardization of the elements leads to the formation of an additive group theme; the group takes over the function of the individual elements." [08]

In the 1950s, the manager of the Globus Zürich department store group, Hans Mahler, founded the ABM Warenhauskette based on the "low-price store model." [06] Comparable models were EPA in Switzerland, Kaufhalle in Germany, Monoprix in France, and Standa in Italy. It experienced its greatest success under Georges Cavelti, who managed the ABM Warenhauskette from 1963 to 1989.

Its visual identity is based on elementary geometrical forms: the circle, square, and rectangle. For a series of products, an area is composed of one of the geometric forms represented in two similar colors, and thus exhibits a main criteria of systematization: reciprocal relationships spanning the related forms and colors. The combinations are nearly infinite, as one of the two aspects — form or color — remains constant as the other is altered.

For ABM Warenhauskette, Eugen Gomringer transforms "concrete poetry" into advertising copy: "The familiar grammar of our written language is reflected and designed in visual and two-dimensional combinations and links and thus takes on increased significance…. With the concrete, design has a new rational foundation: in place of, or more correctly, for the optical experience of the feeling, there is now the awareness of thinking…. The fascination lay with the systemic: designing programs instead of individual solutions, elementary construction kits for exhibition, window display, packaging, typeface, and typography. The aim was to invent design rules: the formula shapes the form. The serial, the repertoire of combinatorics: permutation, combination, and variation are the basic canon of design." [07]

Visual identity by Ernst and Ursula Hiestand (www.hiestanddesign.ch).

Project period: since 1961

[06] Georges Cavelti, ed., ABM: Erfolgsgeschichte einer Warenhauskette, p. 6.   [07] Urs Fanger, in: ibid., p. 141.   [08] Richard Paul Lohse, in Lohse lesen, p. 215.

AUCH MÄNNER MÖGEN ABM!

141-A-8510

Thuisstad
Plezierstad
Perifere stad
Steden van Erasmus
Vitale stad
Transparante stad

Home City
Pleasure City
Peripheral City
City of Erasmus
Vital City
Transparent City

Rotterdam is
many cities

Combinations

1/1
1/2
1/3
1/9
1/27

Rotterdam

Rotterdam

Theme

Cities

City

Rotterdam 2001, Culture Capital of Europe

(Case Study 17)

In 2001, the title "Culture Capital of Europe" was bestowed on the cities of Oporto and Rotterdam. Rotterdam describes itself as a city with incomparable vitality. "It is a city of travellers and explorers, adventurers and discoverers.... More than a hundred languages and more than a hundred and fifty cultures are to be found in this city of culture.... It is a city of many faces, many dimensions. Rich yet poor, cheerful yet sombre, highly ambitious yet too plodding, safe but also feared, beautiful but also ugly — Rotterdam is all of these." [09] "Rotterdam is a city constantly in motion. Transitions which the city has experienced and is experiencing provide challenge and meaning to a year as a cultural capital. A city such as Rotterdam, characterised by intense and rapid processes towards heterogeneity, must continuously ask itself what are the options and possibilities to bind the growing diversity together." [10]

The theme "Rotterdam is many cities" makes reference to Italo Calvino's novel "Invisible Cities," in which Marco Polo tells emperor Kublai Khan stories about the many cities he has visited. In truth, however, he describes one single city in different ways. Rather than Marco Polo, Bert van Meggelen, director of Foundation Rotterdam 2001, narrates various parallel stories about, rather than Venice, Rotterdam. He calls it Pleasure City, You, The City, Vital City, Young@Rotterdam, Home Town, Working City, Peripheral City, Harbours & Domains, City of the Future, Flowing City. The stories raise the issue of the interdependency between individual and group as well as the heterogeneity of the city with its conflicts and synergies. They describe the dissolution of city boundaries and the urban sprawl of cities in the present day. One of the two constant figures in the visual identity is a circular area: the map symbol for "city." [Fig. 1, p. 142] The other is a square with the same basic area. Both figures are depicted in various

[09] Rotterdam 2001, Culturele Hoofdstad van Europa, Programma 2001, p. 7.   [10] Ibid., p. 19.   143

proportions: 1:1, 1:2, 1:3, 1:9, and 1:27, whereby the individual
form is increasingly transformed into a halftone pattern area.
The grid areas also each take up the same basic area. This dissolution can be read as a reference to the fissuring and fragmenta-
tion of cities. [Fig. 2, p. 142] All elements and combinations can
appear in both positive and negative forms. In addition, the colors
green, magenta, and blue, as well as black, appear; other color
variations result from overprinting the colored areas. The typeface, Berthold Akzidenz Grotesk, supports the simple and clear
language of the visual identity. The logo appears in three color
variations. [Fig. 2, p. 145]
In all variations, the basic forms are used rather freely and playfully. A heterogeneous overall picture is created from the various combinations of form and color that, in spite of its complexity, does not appear to be so.

Visual identity by Armand Mevis and Linda van Deursen. Year of origin: 2000

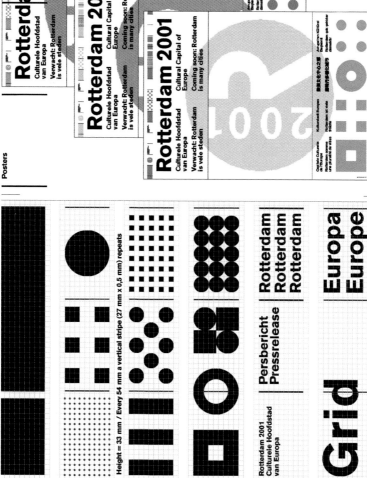

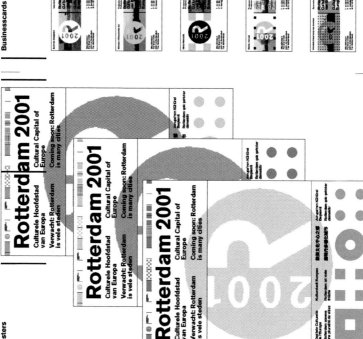

Rotterdam 2001

Culturele Hoofdstad van Europa

Cultural Capital of Europe

Verwacht: Rotterdam is vele steden

Coming soon: Rotterdam is many cities

Height = 33 mm / Every 54 mm a vertical stripe (27 mm x 0,5 mm) repeats

Rotterdam 2001 Culturele Hoofdstad van Europa

Persbericht Pressrelease

Rotterdam Rotterdam Rotterdam

Europa Europe

Grid

Cityplanning 1980 2001

Rotterdam 2001
Culturele Hoofdstad
van Europa

Las Palmas

Rotterdam in Motion

Reading 'Charlene'
Interpictorial Dialogue
Kelly vs Johns

Havens & Heerlijkheden

Rotterdam 2001
Culturele Hoofdstad
van Europa

2001

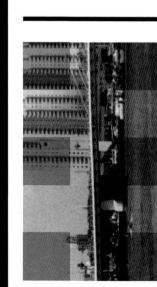

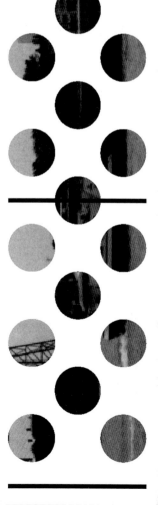

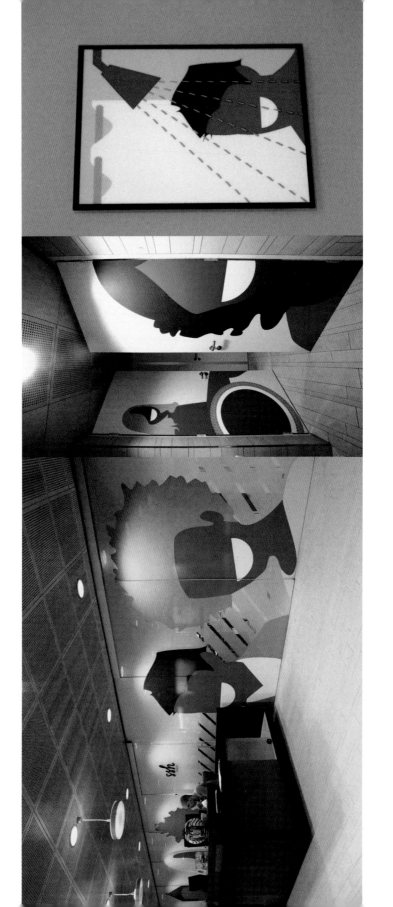

SSH Utrecht

(Case Study 18)

Family resemblances

Wittgenstein describes the term "family resemblances" [Familienähnlichkeit] as follows: "We see a complicated network of similarities overlapping and criss-crossing: sometimes overall similarities, sometimes similarities of detail.... I can think of no better expression to characterize these similarities than 'family resemblances'; for the various resemblances between members of a family: build, features, colour of eyes, gait, temperament, etc., etc. overlap and criss-cross in the same way." [11]

The sign families or language-like visual identities described in this investigation might also be characterized with this description. The visual identity of SSH Utrecht presents elements that belong to the same family; the network of similarities between background, hair, face, and clothes is uncanny. Wittgenstein's description however does not state that a family has one feature present in all instances, which is the case here: all characters have the same mouth. For this and other reasons, it is not a strict case of family resemblance.

The SSH Utrecht, a social housing organization, is part of the University of Utrecht and oversees approximately 8,200 rooms and apartments throughout the city. The tenants are a generation of students characterized by incredibly diverse cultural and family backgrounds, and yet within SSH Utrecht they form a kind of apartment-sharing community or "family," although one that is dispersed — commensurate with our time — throughout the city. Consequently, the relationship between individual and community also plays a central role in the visual identity.

The constant figure in the visual identity is a passport-like portrait of a person representing a single member of the "family." Three portraits of different character form the basic logo. Each portrait is comprised of four saturated fields of color corresponding to the background, hair, face, and clothes. This standard is supported by a recognizable design trait: the bold depiction reduces the characters to pictograms. The portraits have the same mouth; the strongest individual element is the hairstyle, which varies in each character.

The portrait serves the entire gamut of communication media, in which the basic figure and its respective features are modified to a greater or lesser degree. Repeated in the various media, as a whole the characters have a stabilizing effect. The coherence is the result of the net-like references between the four different visual fields: background, hairstyle, face, and clothing, which, through permutation, produce a remarkable number of different possible combinations and thus additional characters.

New characters, however, also generate specific connections to particular situational contexts, such as when a person in a wheelchair features on an orientation sign. For publicizing singular events, such as the inauguration of the new De Bisschoppen (The bishops) building, a thematically relevant solution is found; and

[11] Ludwig Wittgenstein, Philosophical Investigations, pp. 27–28 (§66–7).

because the similar characters produce a stabilizing effect, the new character is immediately recognized as belonging to the sign family despite a strong modification. Because of its thematic relevance, the divergence draws more attention to the singular event than would a basic logo that works at a higher level of universality.

"The design concept allows the client to extend the logo family with new characters, based on actual portraits of students. Thus, each student can be given his or her own SSH logo, thereby encouraging identification with SSH Utrecht." [12] The visual identity not only communicates symbolically the basic theme of "individuality and community," it is a part of what constitutes "individuality and community" within the SSH Utrecht organization. This visual identity illustrates the potential of well-thought and well-designed flexible visual identities. Variation allows the inclusion of ever more characters of diverse social and cultural backgrounds in a differentiated way. These differences can make a visual identity richer and brings it closer to reality, and thus, seen from inside as well as outside, affords diverse possibilities for identification: a differentiated message contributes to a differentiated image of society.

Visual identity by Studio Dumbar. Year of origin: 2005

Reciprocal References

Fig. 1, p. 150: In this sequence, interrelations develop through like, similar, and contrasting coloring within a constant form. The schematic drawing of the T-shirts is particularly well suited for displaying the variety of combination possibilities.

[12] Studio Dumbar, www.studiodumbar.com.

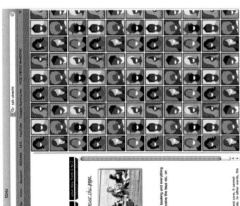

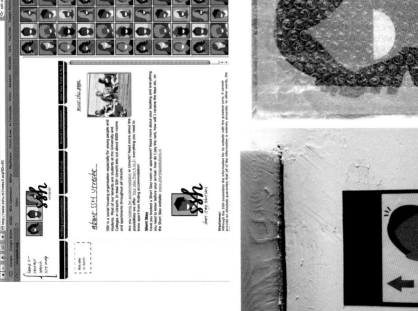

OPENINGSFEEST DE BISSCHOPPEN

woe 20 juni vanaf 17.00 uur

Meine Nachbarin ist alkoholkrank.

Alkoholprobleme gehen uns alle an.
Reden wir darüber!

Wir bieten Unterstützung:
www.sfa-ispa.ch
Tel. 021 321 29 15

sfa / ispa
Schweizerische Fachstelle für Alkohol-
und andere Drogenprobleme

Meine Mutter ist alkoholkrank.

Alkoholprobleme gehen uns alle an.
Reden wir darüber!

Wir bieten Unterstützung:
www.sfa-ispa.ch
Tel. 021 321 29 15

sfa / ispa
Schweizerische Fachstelle für Alkohol-
und andere Drogenprobleme

Mein Mann ist alkoholkrank.

Alkoholprobleme gehen uns alle an.
Reden wir darüber!

Wir bieten Unterstützung:
www.sfa-ispa.ch
Tel. 021 321 29 15

sfa / ispa
Schweizerische Fachstelle für Alkohol-
und andere Drogenprobleme

Mein bester Freund ist alkoholkrank.

Alkoholprobleme gehen uns alle an.
Reden wir darüber!

Wir bieten Unterstützung:
www.sfa-ispa.ch

sfa / ispa
Schweizerische Fachstelle für Alkohol-
und andere Drogenprobleme

Mein Vater ist alkoholkrank.

Alkoholprobleme gehen uns alle an.
Reden wir darüber!

Wir bieten Unterstützung:
www.sfa-ispa.ch

sfa / ispa
Schweizerische Fachstelle für Alkohol-
und andere Drogenprobleme

Mein Sohn ist alkoholkrank.

Alkoholprobleme gehen uns alle an.
Reden wir darüber!

Wir bieten Unterstützung:
www.sfa-ispa.ch

sfa / ispa
Schweizerische Fachstelle für Alkohol-
und andere Drogenprobleme

A Problem with Many Faces

In 2006, the SFA — Schweizerische Fachstelle für Alkohol- und andere Drogenprobleme (Swiss Institute for the Prevention of Alcoholism and other Drug Dependencies) — launched for the first time a national campaign to support those suffering from alcohol abuse as well as their relatives and loved ones. Its aim is to stimulate discussion in society: "Alcohol problems affect us all — let's talk about it."

In each campaign, the posters employ four different motifs. In the background of the posters can be seen a person out of focus representing the alcoholic; in the foreground is a person in focus looking into the camera. Each poster features a different constellation: in 2006, a young woman and her husband, a young woman and her mother, a young man and his boss, and an older gentleman and his neighbor; in 2007, a woman and her son, a girl and her father, a young man and his best friend, and a man and his wife. Without the variations, the problem would be represented in a considerably more general fashion: the person in the background would stand for "the alcoholics" and the one in the foreground for "the relatives." With the variations, however, it is possible to depict age and gender in a more differentiated way, as well as highlight different relationships — relatives, work colleagues, neighbors.

The consistent image composition makes the connection between the campaign and the organization easy to remember, and the variations cause viewers to do a double-take and once again take note of the motif. The campaign provides different possibilities for identification: it aims at the heart of the question of alcohol abuse and its drawn-out emotional processes, while acknowledging that there are no simple and immediate solutions.

Poster series by a working group made up of SFA representatives (www.sfa-ispa.ch) and Atelier Grand, Sierre (www.jmgrand.ch). Project period: 2006–2007

Figs. 1–6, p. 154 and figs. 1–2, p. 155:
SFA poster series

Summary

Variability becomes dynamic when the variation of the elements
is further reinforced by their combination. The elements enter
into a conspicuous coherence, into a reference system. The visual
identity of the Aktau Marina Residential District, Kazakhstan, is
based on the parallel application of varied patterns; collectively,
the impression of texture dominates over that of the individual
ornament. Appropriate for Kazakhstan, the distinctive feature of
diverse patterns and textures partially layered as carpet-like
surfaces transforms an everyday location, such as a street or a
parking lot, into a richly furnished scene.

What distinguishes modules and modular systems? The distinction can be imagined as follows: a module is like a Lego brick
with plugs on one side and matching openings on the other. This
plug connection makes possible a wide range of parallel or
angular combinations, also with other kinds of modules such as
angle modules, straight modules, etc. The laws of construction
prescribe the specific aesthetics. In the modular design for the
detergent packaging of Teddymat, Teddy 75, and Roby 75, the
interfaces between the waves correspond to the plugs, which
represent docking possibilities for the waves on the packages.
In the visual identity of the Cité Internationale Universitaire de
Paris, to be discussed in chapter 5, the angular form of the basic
logo facilitates the logos of the sub-visual identities — here the
different houses of the Cité Internationale. [Fig. 1, p. 161] The building block, however, is a simpler module, on a more elementary
level. While also having a fixed form, it must be combined with
the appropriate "bonding agents," and is thus more flexible in
its combinations.

Arranging different elements in a modular system causes the
simplification of the individual elements: elementary basic
forms are best suited to mutual combination. In a system, the
individual elements interlace like building blocks, are depend-

ent upon each other, and form a self-contained whole. The cohesion between elements is based on connections described by Karl Gerstner as "natural," upon which the laws of geometry and color theory are founded, and part from the supposition that visual elements are continuous. Coherence is also created due to the fact that in each case one of the parameters remains stable — e. g., the form — while another is varied — e. g., the color, as with the ABM Warenhauskette visual identity. A similar dynamic is at work in the visual identity of SSH Utrecht, but differs in that there are more intermediate stages on the level of form — principally the person's hairstyle — and of color.

A general trend can be seen very clearly in the visual identity of SSH Utrecht: the similarity between sign and organization is proportional to the similarities between the signs. At the core of the spectrum are many similar signs whose characteristics, closely related to the organization, assume a stabilizing function. As one moves towards the outer area of the spectrum, the signs' reference to the organization decreases, and at the limit of the spectrum the signs display great difference. These signs represent the specific, the temporary, or the context-specific — in the case of SSH Utrecht it is the poster for the opening of a new building, De Bisschoppen. Stabilizing and specifying functions are not fulfilled by variable elements, but by the complementary aspect of signs.

05.
Element and Structure:
Permutation

What design possibilities does the future hold? Will new methodologies emerge in the field of flexible visual identities? A discussion of different approaches in the following two chapters will reveal certain trends. Future design potential lies in interdisciplinary workgroups benefitting from the possibilities offered by perpetually updateable databases and generative archives, and in custom-designed computer programs and sub-programs (plugins), as evidenced in the case studies of the Twin Cities and the Cité Internationale Universitaire de Paris. In the future, programs developed to control and design ongoing processes will take the place of closed visual identities.

This chapter will also examine methods of combination. While the previous chapter discussed the trend of designers combining fewer elemental figures, here we deal with a considerably larger number of elements of more complex form combined via a computer keyboard. The visual identity for Cité Internationale is based on the assignation of groups of characters from other writing systems to respective Roman characters; a random generator selects the characters from the groups and distributes them throughout the typeface. Rather than characters, in the visual identity of the Walker Art Center, terms are combined, which can be deposited into variable patterns and, sequentially, function as signifying "strips" for the center. The visual identity of Flughafen Köln-Bonn is based on the permutation of visual signs, which are depicted in various degrees of abstraction. In all three cases, the computer program has a central function in determining the sequence of signs, even though these are first designed by hand.

Cité Internationale Universitaire de Paris
(Case Study 19)

The Cité Internationale Universitaire de Paris is in the 14th arrondissement of Paris and is an international residential estate accommodating around 5,500 students, researchers, scientists, and artists. Founded in 1925 with the support of industrial benefactors, bankers, and foreign foundations, the Cité Internationale is made up of forty different buildings, each of which is, as a general norm, associated with a particular nation. Half of the residents are of the nationality of the respective house, while the other half is made up of other nationalities. The Cité Internationale has its own theatre and orchestra and is host to a wide range of student groups for sport, art, and culture. At present, people from more than 120 countries are living and working at Cité Internationale. In addition to French, English, German, Spanish, Italian, Dutch, Danish, Portuguese, and Norwegian, other languages spoken at Cité Internationale include Chinese, Japanese, Vietnamese, Greek, Russian, Arabic, Hindi, and Farsi; such a broad range of languages results in the presence of diverse writing systems, such as the Latin, Cyrillic, Greek, Arabic, and Chinese.

The visual appearance is based on the coexistence of diverse written languages as the Latin alphabet is expanded with typographical characters of other cultures. The typographical raw material, the Newut Plain font by André Baldinger — particularly suitable for the similarity in size of the lower- and uppercase letters — was systematically expanded by the addition of fifty-seven characters from other writing systems, a grouping of which is assigned to each letter. The typographical variation correlates not to individual sentences, as described in chapter 3, but implemented for almost every letter, which, due to formal similarities, can be read in combination with the Latin alphabet. When we read a text we do not read letter by letter but rather our eyes scan

Is Language the Permutation of Letters?

"Could language overcome typography using its own system?" [01] asks Andrew Blauvelt, designer of the visual identity of the Walker Art Center. Starting from the Greek word "stoicheion," which unites the meanings of "element," "atom," and "letter" [02], in his essay "Zu den Elementen" (On the elements) Franz Josef Czernin developed the idea that, viewed soberly, one could "assign to poetry a designated material understood as a finite number of clearly distinguishable units." [03] He is thus saying that language, even poetry, is based on the combination and permutation of elements — sounds, letters, syllables, and words. It seems outrageous to attribute the infinite combinations of language to the permutation of its components, but it nevertheless helps us to understand the principle of the visual identities in this chapter. We find in all three visual identities elements assembled into structures whose connections are loose constellations that can be continuously rearranged. "The typographer 'sets.' He sets individual letters into words,

    [01] Andrew Blauvelt, Walker Expanded, http://design.walkerart.org/detail.wac?id=2090&title=Featured%20Project
[02] Franz Josef Czernin, Elemente, Sonette, p. 145.   [03] Ibid.

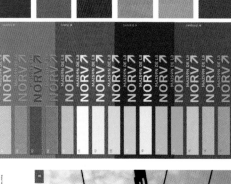

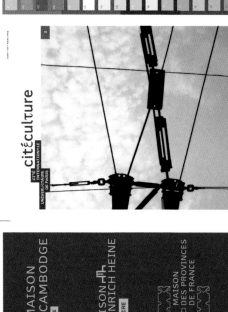

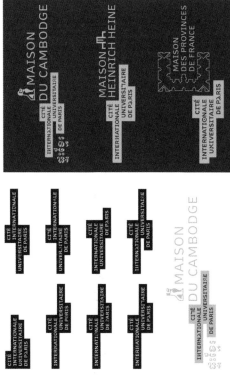

citéculture

CITÉ INTERNATIONALE UNIVERSITAIRE DE PARIS

légère

une des premières habitations collectives conçue par le corbusier, la fondation suisse. lui a permis d'expérimenter certains de ses principes d'architecture et d'urbanisme. le bâtiment est ainsi composé de trois blocs distincts qui correspondent à différentes fonctions (logements, espaces collectifs, circulation); une barre de quatre niveaux repose sur six grands pilotis abrite les chambres; une aile courbe d'un seul niveau contient les espaces collectifs; un module UNE DES PREMIÈRES HABITATIONS COLLECTIVES CONÇUE PAR LE D'ARCHITECTURE ET D'URBANISME. LE BÂTIMENT EST AINSI COMPOSÉ DE TROIS BLOCS DISTINCTS QUI CORRESPONDENT A DIFFÉRENTES FONCTIONS (LOGEMENTS, ESPACES COLLECTIFS, CIRCULATION); UNE BARRE DE QUATRE NIVEAUX REPOSANT SUR SIX GRANDS PILOTIS ABRITE LES CHAMBRES; UNE AILE COURBE D'UN SEUL NIVEAU CONTIENT LES ESPACES COLLECTIFS; UN MODULE PLUS PETIT ET ETROIT, DE

QUATRE NIVEAUX, ACCOLE AU BLOC EST DESTINE

forte

une des premières habitations collectives conçue par le corbusier, la fondation suisse. lui a permis d'expérimenter certains de ses principes d'architecture et d'urbanisme. le bâtiment est ainsi composé de trois blocs distincts qui correspondent à différentes fonctions (logements, espaces collectifs, circulation); une barre de quatre niveaux repose sur six grands pilotis abrite les chambres; une aile courbe d'un seul niveau contient les espaces collectifs; un module UNE DES PREMIÈRES HABITATIONS COLLECTIVES CONÇUE PAR LE D'ARCHITECTURE ET D'URBANISME. LE BÂTIMENT EST AINSI COMPOSÉ DE TROIS BLOCS DISTINCTS QUI CORRESPONDENT A DIFFÉRENTES FONCTIONS (LOGEMENTS, ESPACES COLLECTIFS, CIRCULATION); UNE BARRE DE QUATRE NIVEAUX REPOSANT SUR SIX GRANDS PILOTIS ABRITE LES CHAMBRES; UNE AILE COURBE D'UN SEUL NIVEAU CONTIENT LES ESPACES COLLECTIFS; UN MODULE PLUS PETIT ET ETROIT, DE

QUATRE NIVEAUX, ACCOLE AU BLOC EST DESTINE

words into sentences. Letters are the elementary particles of the written language — and thus of typography. They are figurative signs for sounds without content, parts which acquire a meaning and a value only if they are combined. This means that combinations of two, three, and more letters show in any case a word-picture, but definite letters render a definite idea only in a certain sequence; literally they constitute a word. To clarify the example from the other angle, let us take the four letters I D M N which can be combined in twenty-four different ways. From this we can see that only one combination makes the envisaged word MIND. The twenty-three remaining are indeed both legible and pronounceable, they contain the same elements and give the same total. But they do not constitute a linguistic whole. They remain meaningless." [04]

the page of the book, our vision picking out not only syllables or words but whole groups of words and sentences. When designing text, being conscious of how the reading process works enables the intervention in its structure and eliminates the need to reproduce text in its exact linearity. Within a chain of elements are positions that can be altered without intrinsically disturbing the chain: within a word, neither the beginning nor end position may be changed, nor two adjacent elements, otherwise the "sentence" would break up. Foreign elements can then be distributed within this structure of positions.

The distribution has the strongest effect when carried out at random, as it is with the visual identity of Cité Internationale. Leaving the selection to chance not only makes economic sense; as a program controls the distribution, whenever text is written novel arrangements are generated automatically, thus producing a nearly infinite range of variations as the characters are slightly altered in each new combination. The user can choose between two strengths that determine how intensively the typeface will be intermingled with foreign characters. [Fig. 3, p. 161]

Visual identity by Ruedi Baur (artistic direction), Éric Jourdan, Karim Sabano (industrial design), Denis Coueignoux, Béryl de la Grandière, and Ilka Flora (graphic design), Intégral Ruedi Baur et associés, Paris; in collaboration with André Baldinger (typeface development and typography, www.ambplus.com) and LettError (programming of the random generator, www.letterror.com). Project period: 2000–2004

[04] Karl Gerstner, Designing Programmes, p. 58.

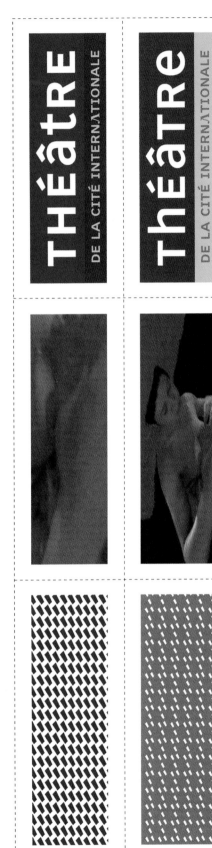

THÉÂTRE
DE LA CITÉ INTERNATIONALE

THÉÂTRE
DE LA CITÉ INTERNATIONALE

THÉÂTRE
DE LA CITÉ INTERNATIONALE

THÉÂTRE
DE LA CITÉ INTERNATIONALE

THÉÂTRE
DE LA CITÉ INTERNATIONALE

SIGNATURE + FOND + DESSIN

THÉÂTRE
DE LA CITÉ INTERNATIONALE

THÉÂTRE
DE LA CITÉ INTERNATIONALE

THÉÂTRE
DE LA CITÉ INTERNATIONALE

THÉÂTRE
DE LA CITÉ INTERNATIONALE

THÉÂTRE
DE LA CITÉ INTERNATIONALE

FOND + SIGNATURE + DESSIN

THÉÂTRE
DE LA CITÉ INTERNATIONALE

THÉÂTRE
DE LA CITÉ INTERNATIONALE

THÉÂTRE
DE LA CITÉ INTERNATIONALE

THÉÂTRE
DE LA CITÉ INTERNATIONALE

THÉÂTRE
DE LA CITÉ INTERNATIONALE

DESSIN + SIGNATURE – FOND

Walker Art Center

(Case Study 20)

The Walker Art Center in Minneapolis was reopened in April 2005 after a modernizing expansion by the architectural studio Herzog & de Meuron. Its special architectonic feature is a metal façade which, depending on how it falls, reflects light in different ways to thus generate a wide range of patterns. In addition to its continuously expanding collection, the Walker Art Center offers a lively program: talks, discussions, and readings; theatre, film, music, and performance art; and gallery, architectural, and garden tours. All these activities are put into a wider context on its website, linked to related activities and discussed on the center's blogs. The Walker Art Center sees itself in equal measure as a "catalyst" for artists and a platform for the involvement of the public: "The Walker Art Center, a catalyst for the creative expression of artists and the active engagement of audiences, examines the questions that shape and inspire us as individuals, cultures, and communities." [05]
"It's (the Walker Art Center) so flexible that I don't have one logo in my mind. Instead, I get an impression, or an approach, or a general vibe. And with the Walker, that was always the idea, as with the Carter commission — the Walker can't make a logo that is going to sum it all up." [06]

The visual identity is based on the Walker typeface designed by Matthew Carter for the center in 1995. There is already a certain flexibility in the font: it includes five different forms of serifs — "snap-on multi-form serifs" — which can be variably added to the characters. "I looked at the Walker typeface wherein a keystroke does not necessarily yield the expected character. What if a character could produce not a letter but an entire word? What role would fonts have in such a scheme?" [07]
Ornamental elements are used alongside text elements: single color areas or patterns threaded together like a string of pearls.

Relationship Networks / Force Fields and Language

"The author Eugen Gomringer says: 'The constellation, the word-group, replaces the verse. Instead of syntax it is sufficient to allow 2, 3 or more words to achieve their full effect. They seem on the surface without interrelation and sprinkled at random by a careless hand, but looked at more closely, they become the centre of a field of force and define a certain scope. In finding, selecting and putting down these words he creates "thought-objects" and leaves the task of association to the reader, who becomes a collaborator and, in a sense, often the completer of the poem.'... Gomringer calls himself the 'play-leader, the one who invites others to play with him'. The words he puts down are not words applied to some subject, but a reality, conceptual and rhythmical values in themselves. They are again and again points in relationship to one another in a vacuum in which the reader's imagination wanders." [08]
In the introduction to "Designing Programmes," Paul Grediger writes, "Thus, for instance, there is a formula

[05] Walker Art Center, http://info.walkerart.org/about/contact.wac#Mission. [06] Eric Olsen, Walker Expanded, http://design.walkerart.org/detail.wac?id=2090&title=Featured%20Project. [07] Andrew Blauvelt, ibid. [08] Karl Gerstner, Designing Programmes, p. 52.

The "strips" are always recognizable even though the elements forming them are variable, and the center of each is allocated a word field that conveys its specific orientation.

The distinct designs of the strips are executed by computer. A word selected from the respective word group is generated via the appropriate computer key—for example, "D" generates "design," "E" "exhibitions"—and appears in the proper typeface and size and on the chosen ornament. Overlapping represents the greatest technical challenge: "PostScript only allows you to work in a single color. You can't work on the same thing and have different colors that then overlap. That's the limitation of the technology. To get around that obstacle, I actually approached it in a very analogue way. If you break it apart into two bits by using the space bar, change the colors, and then make it one again— by deleting the space — you are able to overlap the pieces and the data is such that it doesn't matter if it is overlapping." [09]

All communication media—from business cards to signage—are designed with the strip. Functioning like "tape" that both wraps around and binds, the visual identity remains at the surface and constant regardless of the chosen medium. The façade projection is an exception: the various strips move against each other to emphasize their "ticker tape character," which is then represented in print versions with a full-bleed. [10]

Each department of the Center is allocated a corresponding text field that is integrated into the strips. "One font called Peer to Peer incorporates the language of institutional bureaucracy— the names of departments, for instance — while another one titled Public Address translates some of this language in terms that are more accessible to the general public. For instance, one font represents 'Film/Video' as a department: 'screenings' is a type of event, 'Regis Dialogues' is a specific gateway program unique to that department, and 'movies' is more common parlance. All

in poetry corresponding to this conception. The traditional structure of language is dissolved. No grammar. No syntax. The elements are single words. They stand loose in the line with all their valencies free. The rule of the game is permutation. The poems arising are called constellations. Constellations are a poetic programme." [11]

Although these considerations were formulated in the publication with regard to Eugen Gomringer, they can be read as a description of literary deconstruction processes, whose most important work is the collection of prose "Six Residua" by Samuel Beckett. "Lessness," the last prose piece in "Six Residua," consists of sentences whose components cannot be directly related either syntactically or semantically. The sentences are incomplete in their grammatical structure and can at most be described as fragments in comparison to traditional prose form. Through the serial process of permutation and recurrence, the sentence parts become loose units of meaning stuck together, variations of the same motif. The text material does not permit the recognition of a hierarchical order, and could

[09] Eric Olsen, Walker Expanded, http://design.walkerart.org/detail.wac?id=2090&title=Featured%20Project.
[10] http://blogs.walkerart.org/newmedia/wp-content/uploads/2006/08/hennepin_ave2.mov.
[11] Paul Grediger, introduction, Design Programmes, p. 4.

be read in all conceivable directions; the text is characterized by a dynamic structure. Lessness (Sans) refers to a lack of qualities, everything is "without something": the time and spatial dimension of the world of the "little body" appears almost completely dissolved, the colors have atrophied into a monochrome gray. Anything like a noise is absorbed by complete silence, the world of objects is transformed into ephemeral chimeras. Overall the text arouses the impression of endless distances: earth and sky have melted into one another and thus do not span any real space. Without differences, no movement — the dynamics of the prose is simultaneously its "stasis." The lack (of qualities), as we can also observe in the abstract and elemental, brings to mind the state "before the form" or "after the form." The set word is kept in movement; the text is in an open-ended process, an eternal "becoming."

of these examples relate to one of the many artistic disciplines the Walker presents. The ability to embed the language of all the disciplines in the identity emphasized the unique character of the Walker as a place for all the arts. The vocabularies can grow and change over time. Their use is tied more to context than convention." [12] Word groupings form a close semantic relationship to a specific department and its distinct public, and can react to changes such as the development of new departments, special programs, and even specific events. "It is quite possible to take data from actual surveys and use it to create such a vocabulary. In a way, this new identity becomes its own little record of institutional change over time." [13]

Visual identity by Andrew Blauvelt and Chad Kloepfer; in collaboration with Eric Olson (programming of the fonts), Scott Ponik (design: Walker Membership and Gallery Cards [fig. 4, p. 167]), and Walker Design Department (Design Walker Calendar 2005 [figs. 1–2, p. 172]). Year of origin: 1997

[12] Andrew Blauvelt, Walker Expanded, http://design.walkerart.org/detail.wac?id=2090&title=Featured%20Project.   [13] Ibid.

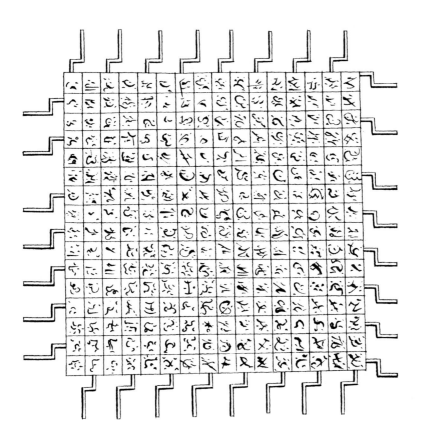

The Modularity of Knowledge

"When Captain Gulliver visited the Grand Academy of Lagado, he saw 'a frame … twenty foot square … in the middle of the room. The superficies was composed of several bits of wood about the bigness of a die … linked together by slender wires … covered on every square with paper … and on these papers were written all the words of their language … The pupils … took each of them hold on an iron handle … and giving them a sudden turn the whole disposition of the words was entirely changed … The professor showed me several volumes in large folio already collected, of broken sentences … and out of those rich materials (he intended) to give the world a complete body of all arts and sciences …'" [14]

Fig. 1, p. 173: A utopian machine for the generation of knowledge through a combination of its modules.

[14] Phillip Morrison, The Modularity of Knowing, p. 1.

Flughafen Köln-Bonn

(Case Study 21)

Flughafen Köln-Bonn (Cologne-Bonn Airport) is located in
Cologne's southeastern outskirts, and is "in the general proximity of two large airports" [15]: Frankfurt and Dusseldorf. "Further
development is not a question of infringing on the territory of our
competitors, but finding arguments the others cannot put for-
ward: simplicity and easy accessibility, low prices, demythifica-
tion of the airport, and the creation of a pleasant transitional
space." [16] These qualities culminate in the themes of reduction,
flexibility, and playfulness conveyed by the visual identity.

The airport's typeface — SimpleKölnBonn — is a derivation of
Simple, a monotype font characterized by its uniform line width.
To supplement the characters, Atelier Norm developed a spectrum of pictograms, the SimpleKölnBonnSymbols, which can be
inserted directly from the keyboard. The color spectrum starts
out from a light blue, frequently used for airports, and is extended
with five other colors — yellow, green, orange, gray, and black.
All the colors can be combined with each other and mixed to produce a darker spectrum. The employment of people in silhouette
forms a contrast to the pictograms and, being substantially more
differential, allow the representation of more complex information, such as nationality.
The visual identity is based on these constant elements, which
appear in varying constellations as well as varying local contexts.
The conventional way of reading is thereby shifted and variations
in meaning produced.
The pictogram is the protagonist and all other signs relate to it
and its specific semantic and syntactic qualities. The meaning of
a pictogram is revealed by its resemblance to the signified, to
what is being designated, and also by convention. A part of this
convention is the local and temporal reference: the syntax of
the sign. The pictogram of a woman is only understood in the

 [15] Jean Michel Place, ed., Köln Bonn Airport: corporate design / Intégral Ruedi Baur et associés, 2003.
[16] Ibid.

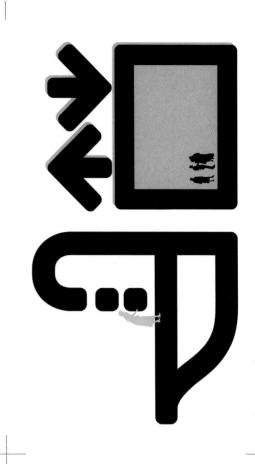

Bildsprache

Nicht.

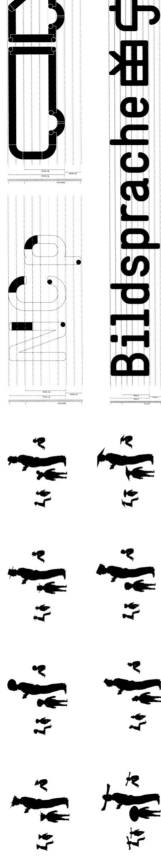

In Deutschland gibt es rund 120.000 Vermögensmillionäre. Sie gelten als die Reichen im Lande. Damit sind ihnen zwei Dinge ganz sicher: Neid und immer neue Begehrlichkeiten des Fiskus. Wer da glaubt, von einer Million als Bonvivant gut leben zu können, der kennt das deutsche Steuerrecht schlecht. Stellen wir uns den steuerehrlichen Herrn Michel vor, der eine Million erarbeitet oder geerbt hat. Vielleicht ist er ein Winzer, der sich zur Ruhe gesetzt und die Weinberge verkauft hat, vielleicht ist er auch ein in die Jahre gekommener Handwerker oder Zahnarzt. Jedenfalls will Herr Michel, da er keine weiteren Einkünfte hat, von dieser Million leben. Er beschließt also: keine Segeljacht in Marbella und keine Villa im Tessin. Vielmehr legt er seine Million in festverzinslichen Wertpapieren an. Dazu wählt er zum Beispiel Bundesobligationen. Der Staat bietet ihm für diese fünfjährigen Papiere zur Zeit 6,09 Prozent. Herr Michel bekommt also 60.900 DM brutto im Jahr. Nun macht Herr Michel seine Steuererklärung, verrechnet den Zinsabschlag mit seiner Einkommensteuerbelastung, macht Freibeträge geltend, nutzt abzugsfähige Sonderausgaben und den Altersentlastungsbeitrag. Mit einigem Geschick reduziert er sein zu versteuerndes Einkommen so auf nur mehr 45.000 DM. Darauf hat er dann knapp 10.500 DM Steuern zu zahlen. Es bleiben ihm von seinem Zinsertrag also 50.400 DM übrig. Doch damit nicht genug. Nun wird der treuen Michel — er hat schließlich ein Vermögen — noch Vermögensteuer abverlangt. Wieder nutzt er alle Freibeträge, reduziert sein steuerpflichtiges Vermögen auf 920.000 DM, und doch greift der Fiskus kräftig zu. Wenn es nach den neuesten Plänen der Regierung geht, muß Michel ein Prozent des Gesamtbetrages zahlen. Für ihn bedeutet das, noch einmal 9.200 DM an den Staat zu überweisen. Seine Bilanz: Für die Million Anlagekapital in Bundesobligationen behält er am Ende 41.200 DM Zinsertrag übrig — genausoviel wie die Inflationsrate, die derzeit Michels D-Mark entwertet. Das Fazit: Der steuerliche Millionär muß unter den gegenwärtigen Umständen froh sein, wenn er keinen realen Vermögensverlust erleidet. In Deutschland gibt es rund 120.000 Vermögensmillionäre. Sie

Determinedly
Undetermined

When dynamic networks of relationships are represented with static
means, the essentials of flexible relationships remain invisible. The most
complex graphic representations of
such networks, composed of dots
joined by lines, are left essentially as
ornament, as it is a question of references between the diverse thematic
levels rather than between the individual dots. In addition, the relationships are more undetermined than
the static networks can indicate.
The scores of contemporary compos-
ers prepare interpreters in the sense
of a set of guidelines consciously
leaving them a great deal of latitude;
the visual arrangement of signs becomes a field of mobile constellations.
John Cage's "Fontana Mix," "consists
of a total of twenty-two pages of
graphic material: ten pages each with
six curved lines as well as ten trans-
parencies with randomly distributed
dots. According to a system defined
by the composer, two such pages are
overlaid with a grid to create inter-
sections, connecting lines and values
which can be freely attributed to

local reference as a "ladies' bathroom," as it would be absurd to
read it that way if seen out of context. If the convention is broken
the meaning disintegrates and, given the circumstances, may
even be redefined by the viewer.

The pictograms are available as a font on the computers of most
of the airport staff, and are tools of external and internal communication. The communication department works with the tools
and the color palette and thus can develop their own individual
color style.

Pictograms have various levels of meaning. The "ascending airplane" pictogram is used in combination with the word "Departure," and may also be found on a large window open to the sky.
[Fig. 2, p. 176] There the literal meaning is dominant: the pictogram
is almost literally read as the picture of an airplane taking off.
Besides the position, size and dimension play a decisive role.
The real object — the airplane that is perhaps flying past in the
moment of perception — places itself in relationship to these
two levels.

A shift between the levels can be seen because various levels of
abstraction are combined. When the suitcase pictogram represents the three-dimensional object "suitcase" [fig. 4, p. 176], there
is an alienating effect produced by the mixture of different levels
of abstraction. Surprising and intriguing references, comic situations, and staged moments form an open reference system of
allusions which can be briefly glimpsed and can provoke new
types of associations.

We also know the effect of the mixture of various levels of abstraction from other visualizations such as maps. There, however, it
occurs due to a functional necessity, the change of scale. In comparison, the game with the mixture of representational levels
is a reaction to the complexity of our reality, which is closely connected to the complexity of media reality.

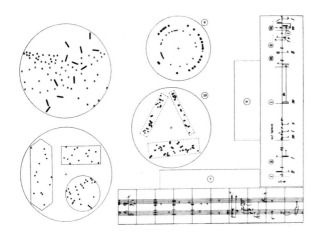

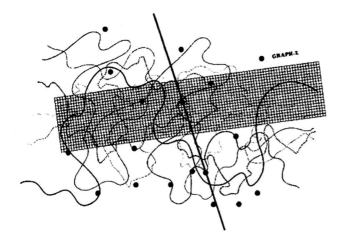

musical qualities such as volume, tone color, and pitch." [17] The composition thus creates decisive conditions where the unpredictable can occur. A new constellation of the score is put together at each performance, whereby the respective moment has an influence on its structure.

Fig. 1, p. 178: Visual score by Mauricio Kagel (Transición II for piano, drums and two tapes), composed as guidelines for spatial and gestural musical actions.

Fig. 2, p. 178: Fontana-Mix

Fig. 1, p. 179: Zollverein School, Essen

Fig. 2, p. 179: Aby Warburg, Mnemosyne-Atlas. "Walter Benjamin (Das Passagen-Werk / The Arcades Project) and Aby Warburg (Mnemosyne-Atlas) developed models in the first half of the twentieth century showing how contingencies and constellations can provide a different kind of access to conveying knowledge and insights textually and pictorially in a traditional terrain." [18]

[17] Martina Sauerwald, www.straebel.de/praxis/text/t-cage-fontana.htm.

[18] Rudolf Frieling, www.medienkunstnetz.de/themes/mapping_and_text/editorial/3/.

The dominance of the pictogram and the playful shifts result in a simplification reminiscent of "Playmobil" or "comics," and thus creates a comical and somewhat ironic level. For example, at the information stand, the presence of a person in front of the enlarged speech bubble has a comic-like effect and, at the same time, creates a visual narrative quality that provides not only coherency, but also cracks and fissures and thus surprise. Perception can be set in motion through the use of various montage techniques, through a shift or change of the level of abstraction, through permutation, and through the mobility of the elements in relation to each other.

Visual identity by Intégral Ruedi Baur et associés, in collaboration with Atelier Norm (typeface development, www.norm.to). Project period: 2002–2006

Figs. 1–3, p. 180 and fig. 1, p. 181: "Poles of Influence"

Poles of Influence

Non-linear, constellation arrangements rouse the viewer to discover a variety of references and reference planes. Wooden poles normally used as supports for banana trees on the island are employed in the work "Poles of Influence" and, arising from the immediate local context, the material all but automatically speaks of the area. The interaction between the "normal" and the emblematic sign is evocative for the viewer on any number of levels, or perhaps the interaction "charges" these familiar objects so as to be redis-covered by the island's inhabitants.

This process strengthens the coher-ence of the work in a quite natural, self-evident manner. The poles are identi-fied with a color-coded system in which each pole is assigned a specific num-ber. The numbers come from different contexts — from license plates to phone numbers of ex-girlfriends — and are installed in groups following a specific matrix across the whole island, thus creating a series of associative possi-bilities which allow both inhabitants and visitors of the island to interweave their own stories with the coordinates. The markings impart to locations of the island a theatrical, scenic relevancy. Does something from the past lie

hidden here? Is something planned here or is an imaginary path indicated? Possible perspectives and interpreta-tions are consciously alluded to, and yet the coherence of the whole seman-tic field is maintained through a net-work of references that produces a coherency among the poles.

Project by Peter Anderson
(www.peterandersonstudio.co.uk).

Year of origin: 2005

Parallel Processing

The catalogue documents the work of the artist Asier Pérez González. He develops his performative projects on the basis of a business model: for every single project he founds a limited company with its own office, appoints appropriate staff, acquires sponsors, and sees himself as the owner-manager of his own artistic activity. For example, for the "Kissarama" project, González, "together with his production company Funky Projects, made an attempt to break the Guinness world record of 1,588 simultaneously kissing pairs, a project of a highly symbolic character in a city which has for years been characterized by war and hostility between two sections of the population." [19] Each of the thirty companies in the catalogue has its own visual identity and is thus easily identifiable within the unusual organizational structure in which the alphabetical order of the projects is subordinate to the order of sub-aspects, including clients, sponsors, organization, and creative output. The projects are thus not treated individually one after the other, but rather addressed based on the particular sub-aspect.

Subdividing an artifact into its sub-aspects inherently opens up diverse design possibilities. The sub-aspects can suggest themes for sign families or be configured in various relations, and, depending on the degree of complexity, can be set in reference to one another or interwoven by creative allusions.

The organizational structure of the catalogue opens for readers a different vision of the artistic oeuvre of Asier Pérez González: it emphasizes the parallelism of his projects and their multi-layered references to each other. In comparison to classic, linear ordering techniques, the structure has the effect of an order "before the order." It not only indicates a highly personal working method, but also reflects a common contemporary experience: projects are rarely developed in sequence; they overlap and permeate, interrupt and fecundate each other. It is rather easy to imagine that while speaking on the phone with the sponsors of project X, Asier Pérez González is thinking of how to respond to the sponsors of project Y. "Nowadays we are actually always working simultaneously in a brainstorming phase, a drafting phase, and a concluding phase in the design process

of various projects. There is no self-contained, linear development process. This illusion can no longer be maintained. We must combine the complex synergies of the parallel force fields with a great deal of improvisation so as not to allow the creativity of the design process to be smothered." [20]

Catalogue by Laurent Lacour and Kiki Schmidt, ade hauser lacour. Year of origin: 2005

Figs. 1-4, p. 183: Pages from the catalogue for Asier Pérez González

    [19] Hildegund Amanshauser, Enjoyable Situations, p. 28.   [20] Andres Bosshard, personal interview, 2008.

Summary

Compared to the combination of modified individual elements
discussed in the previous chapter, in the present chapter can be
seen two substantial distinctions that represent a quantum leap.
First, there are a considerably larger number of signs; and second,
the combination and permutation of these signs, though developed by a designer, is controlled via computer. The same process
can generate modifications as described in chapter 3, thus
enabling variations in form, color, size, or means of representation, such as with the visual identity of Museion, Bozen, where a
constant principle — the "passage-like" — is depicted in various
degrees of abstraction.

Also discussed in this chapter was how pictogram variations
undergo interchangeable permutations, as in the visual identity
of Flughafen Köln-Bonn. The basic approaches to systemization
are intensified many times over as the permutation creates constellations generating reciprocal dynamic references; repeatedly
re-formed by the viewer, in each new constellation the individual
sign varies in meaning and effect. Furthermore, the syntax of the
sign is taken up again in the permutation process, and thus the
sign for "departure" — an ascending airplane in exaggerated
form — can also be found on a window giving onto the sky. The
shift in the semantic and syntactic layer is based on the mixture
of various degrees of abstraction, which, in contrast to a functional application such as map, is playful and theatrical.

All three visual identities discussed in this chapter are based on
the modification of elements of writing-based communication.
The character is combined to form words, words sentences, and
sentences texts; the smaller the variable element, the more varied the combinations formed and the larger the number of variations. The wider the spectrum of typographic and pictographic
variations, the greater is the significance and impact of the visual
identity. It is not a single sign, nor a sign family, but rather the

Summary

The Elementary and the Composite

whole design that has identity-building power. It is basically
thus when working with typographic means. However, in themselves, most typefaces create a reserved, homogenous image
and their use is hardly perceived as "extra." In the visual identity of Cité Internationale, this image is shattered by the use of
modified characters, while the Walker Art Center achieves the
same break through the use of ornamental strips appearing in
conjunction with the words. The dynamic quality of these visual
identities is simultaneously based on an inner stability generated through the system of references between the constellations, which here are primarily reciprocal similarities at the typographic level.

The "elementary" facilitates the production of coherence between two highly heterogeneous aspects. The "self-contained
form" of the elementary basic figures, as used in the visual identities of ABM Warenhauskette and Rotterdam 2001, "makes the
combinations with other elements easy." [21] Here the regulari-
ties of geometry are the foundation for the references. The constant signified of the visual identities of the Cinémathèque française and Quartier des spectacles is "light." "Projected light" as
required for cinema is as a sign something rather elementary,
unlimited, and unspecific; as a sign for "cinema" it becomes more
categorically limited because it is a projection plane. And yet,
"projected light" is a very general sign with which an institution
can hardly be significantly represented. "Elemental" signifies that
something cannot be reduced further. As a visual sign, shining
light possesses inadequate qualities to appear as a significant
sign, and yet this very lack of qualities permits rather diverse
applications, namely variations across diverse media in which the
general signified of light is attributed specific properties.

[21] Wolfgang Schmittel, Process Visual, p. 31.   185

Light becomes specific in projected signs, in elements of the
signage, and in theatrical projections that welcome visitors in the
Cinémathèque foyer. The "elemental quality" of light is further
strengthened by the fact that brightness — alongside form, color,
etc. — is a syntactic aspect of the visual sign. It is as though the
aim was to develop a significant sign with just form.

The spectrum of possible permutations — i. e., variations — of
"light" is evidenced by the two vastly different forms of the visual
identities in which it is employed. While projection is a cinematic
concept, the idea of presentation or concealment by light conveys the scenes and thus the venues of the Quartier des spectacles. As the signifying aspects of the theme of "light" range from
the real to the metaphoric-symbolical to the metaphysical, one
could imagine even more, fundamentally different variations.

The prevailing fields can never be completely disassociated from
one other; their reciprocal perspectives would permeate each
other, and combined they would open up a vast gamut of meaning.
Within the visual identity of the Flughafen Köln-Bonn, the combination of varied means of representation or levels of abstraction
produce great difference. By alternating between pictographic
and photographic depiction, silhouette and real physical object,
the continuous perceptibility of references is called into question.
Here, the elemental form of the pictogram produces the coherency. Similar to "light," the pictogram is highly abstract and concrete at the same time, which is the result of abstracting and
flattening an image that, having had all distinguishing marks re-
moved, appears "un-alive." Combined with other elements, it
reacquires specificity, and, precisely because of its reduced form
and lack of characteristics, provokes the "displacement," "pre-
pared" to associate with other levels of abstraction. This "pre-
paredness" can then generate increasingly new constellations.
Appearing in a constellation with the silhouette weakens the

[22] Ruedi Baur, personal interview, 2006.

functional abstraction of the pictogram and returns to it something special and distinct. The "elevator" pictogram, for example, is thus reduced to its essential functional momentums: two arrows depicting up and down movement and an enclosed area — the abstracted space. In relation with a group of figures, this area takes on spatial depth. [Figs. 1–2, p. 186] And yet, this impression stays with the pictogram only so long as the constellation exists. Relatively featureless at first, at the moment of interaction the pictogram seems to assume the qualities of its collaborator, which influences it without completely combining with it, and thus forms something entirely new.

"I wasn't previously aware that I could evoke this oscillation between the levels of effect and meaning with pictograms, which actually do have a very clear and unambiguous meaning." [22]

06.
Interaction: Control Factors /
Transfer / Open Form

As with the previous chapter, this chapter is devoted to forward-looking approaches, describing flexible visual identities that incorporate in the design real-time processes or data in a dynamic manner; in other words, linking or processing them in real time. Based on a direct link between design and control processes, these visual identities potentiate organizations to not only provide information about their activities but to also simultaneously build identity. Propelled by real processes, the signs have a highly significant and authentic character; these always up-to-date elements prompt more interest than similar yet invariable, designed elements. And yet, at the same time, this form of processual thinking is also the most demanding, as the designer must in some sense deal with an equation with several unknowns.

How can we design something when we are dealing with an open process whose behavior we do not yet know? What means do we need to give public space a substantive image that can interact with the widest range of people? How can we simultaneously realize orientation, identity, and identification potentialities? The visual identity of the Minneapolis-St. Paul metropolitan region — the Twin Cities — is based on a typographic system that reacts to data stemming from the immediate environment, such as wind strength or temperature. The visual identity of Poetry on the Road, an international literary festival, is based on the translation of structural aspects of language. In the visual identity for the Haus der Wissenschaft, Bremen, elements combine in different constellations as a function of variable data from the Internet.

Fig. 1, p. 188: "Tied To Tide"

The Glyph Model

We used a reference system for the type system. It's not difficult to spend hours drawing type, but in order to get a grip of the many variations some sort of direction is necessary.

In the sketch on the right there are 3 categories of parameters. At first we thought it was going to be one-dimensional: an increase in one parameter would mean a decrease in another. Later it became clear that these parameters are not exclusive: it is possible to draw letters which fit in several groups at once. That means that each parameter can be seen as a dimension: the model can be drawn as a cube (far right).

The category names are quite subjective. The goal is not to classify the glyphs as belonging to one or the other, but to quantify each glyph.

Regular / Normal: the model needs some sort of plain reference point. Towards this point all glyphs become increasingly normal. Well, what we consider to be normal. No unusual forms or serifs, a sturdy low contrast sans serif design with subtle curves and rounded edges.

Formal / Serif: a slab serif editing of the Regular / Normal sans. Towards this point all glyphs grow serifs.

Informal / Round: all shapes find curved alternations. Boulder, more handdrawn sometimes receive construction.

Alternate / Weird: the place where all the scary creatures live. Strange and unusual alternations.

...not a one interpolation model!

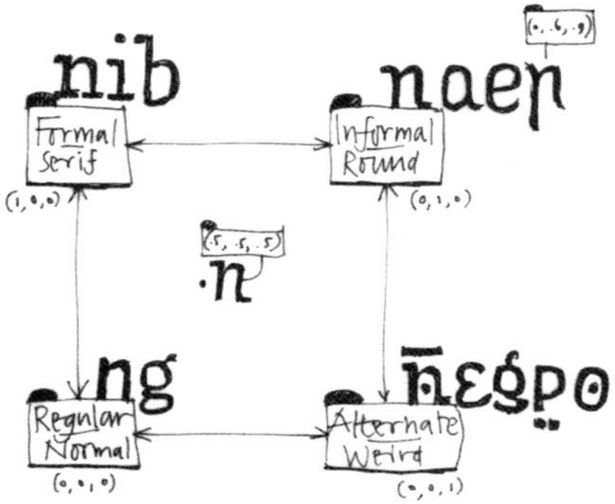

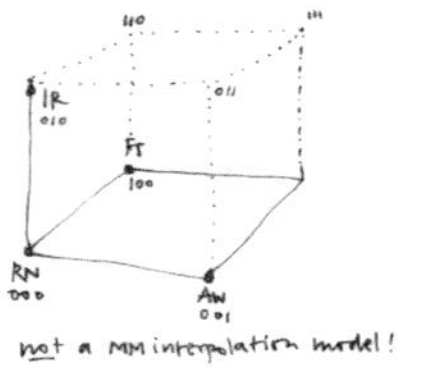

In this model each glyph gets a 3-dimensional coordinate, a point in the cube (x, y, z).

The x-axis is formality, the y-axis is informality (note that formality and informality are not exclusive here). The z-axis is weirdness. Theoretically it is possible to draw a glyph of (1, 1, 1) which should be the formal, informal and alternate/weird all at once. It is not a multiple-master interpolation model!

We're not going to fill all corners of the cube, it's there to be able to enable calculations for the process of glyph selection: 'we need a glyph that's close to (0.75, 0.35, 0.9)!'

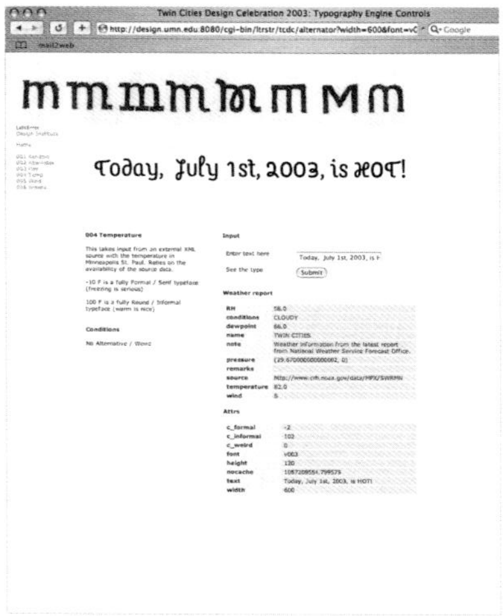

A Typeface for the Twin Cities

(Case Study 22)

Play with the Wind!

For the World New Music Festival 2006 in Stuttgart, the sound artist Andres Bosshard was commissioned to develop a sound tower to record the works presented at the two-week festival and to remix extracts. Brought together into a multilayered composition, the extracts are independent and can be played individually or together in variable sequences; and because the individual sequences of the extracts are interrelated, they have the potential to produce perpetually new variations. Every three minutes a sensor calculates the speed of the wind and selects one of the composition sequences assigned to that speed; if the wind stays the same, the whole composition is played again unchanged.

How can the chaotic behavior of the wind control a composition? Different reference points are assigned to a composition that divide the linear sequence into any number of variations, which are then triggered by predetermined values spontaneously generated by the wind sensor. Thus the unpredictable wind patterns trigger the parts of the composition

In July 2002, the Design Institute of the University of Minnesota invited six design teams to develop a typeface for the Minneapolis-St. Paul metropolitan region. With 3.18 million inhabitants, the region is the sixteenth largest metropolitan area in the United States and, in addition to the twin cities of Minneapolis and St. Paul, includes seven surrounding counties. Behind the name "Twin Cities" is concealed the fact that, although they are increasingly integrated, the two cities retain a strongly independent character. The typeface is intended to reflect this aspect of the Twin Cities. But can a typeface convey the unique and different character of a whole city or such a heterogeneous region?

Twin is not a typeface in the conventional sense, but a system that brings together different typefaces. They demonstrate greater independence than mere type styles because they differ in more ways than simply width and line strength; as a hybrid typeface, the system contains different typefaces with distinct, class-specific characteristics such as a Grotesque and an Antiqua. In addition, the system also integrates ornamental styles and "in-between values." [Fig. 1, p. 190] And yet, all ten typefaces can be recognized as belonging together due to common, form-specific features. One of the biggest challenges was establishing the kerning for over 800 combinable glyphs. "The kerning proved to be a problem. Over 800 glyphs that potentially need to be kerned with each other. Just wrote an autospace/autokern app for the occasion that narrowed it down to 65,420 kerning pairs. Still a lot, but manageable. For the final font releases this was limited even further." [01]

Twin is not a prefabricated element to be used in different implementations, but rather an application that runs on the web with which users can prepare the elements for specific "on the fly" use in an incredibly playful fashion. This application, the "Pan-

[01] LettError, www.letterror.com/portfolio/twin.

1 twin cities design celebration
2 twin cities design celebration
3 twin cities design celebration
4 twin cities design celebration
5 twin cities design celebration
6 twin cities design celebration
7 twin cities design celebration
8 twin cities design celebration

Sans, No strings attached.

The one single same member of the family.

The string sketch from Monty Python's Instant Record Collection Transcribed from tape by Malcolm Dickinson. CLARINET YALE/WIX. 4/5/66. Adrian Wapcaplet: Aah, come in, come in, M...Simpson. Aaah, welcome to Mouseboat, Follicle, Goosecreature, Ampersand, Spong, Wapcaplet, Loosdriver, Vendetta and Prang! Mr. Simpson: Thank you. Wapcaplet: Do sit down—my name's Wapcaplet, Adrian Wapcaplet... Mr. Simpson: how'd'y'do.

†HiⱯ¡†Ha+Bar→→→

aDVer+iⱯing!

shut up & shut your eyes *&%
120,204 Reasons

Annual Report 2004 Mo+E!66

STRINGTITES – JUST THE RIGHT LENGTH!" S: For what? W: "A MILLION HOUSEHOLD USES!" S: Such as? W: Uhmm...Tying up very small parcels, attaching notes to pigeons' legs, uh, destroying household pests. S: Destroying household pests? How? W: Well, if they're

TWIN CITIES DESIGN CELEBRATION 2003

Al's Toy Barn

Foodstuff

American Airlines.

REUTERS + + + Twin Cities Design Celebration. The string sketch from Monty Python's Instant Record Collection Transcribed from tape by Malcolm Dickinson. CLARINET YALE/WIX . 4/5/66. Adrian Wapcaplet: Aah, come in, come in, Mr. Simpson. Aaah, welcome to Mouseboat, Follicle, Goosecreature, Ampersand, Spong, Wapcaplet, Loosdriver, Vendetta and Prang! Mr. Simpson: Thank you. Wapcaplet: Do sit down—my name's Wapcaplet, Adrian Wapcaplet... Mr. Simpson: how'd'y'do. Wapcaplet: Now, Mr. Simpson... Simpson, French, is it? S: No, sir. Ah, now, understand you want us to advertise your washing powder. S: String. W: String, washing powder, what's the difference. We can sell anything. S: Good. Well I have this large quantity of string, a hundred and twenty-two thousand miles of it to be exact, which I inherited, and I thought if I advertised it— W: Of course! A national campaign. Useful stuff, string, no trouble there. S: Ah, but there's a snag, you see. Due to bad planning, the hundred and twenty-two thousand miles is in three inch lengths. So it's not very useful. W: Well, that's our selling point! "SIMPSON'S INDIVIDUAL STRINGETTES!"

FOOD ✶ PHONE ✶ GAS ✶ DIESEL ✶ LODGING

Type&Typography•Fun&Games

Downtowner
LUXURY TAVERNS

The string sketch from Monty Python's Instant Record Collection Transcribed from tape by Malcolm Dickinson. CLARINET YALE/WIX . 4/5/66. Adrian Wapcaplet: Aah, welcome to Mouseboat, Follicle, Goosecreature, Ampersand, Spong, Wapcaplet, Loosdriver, Vendetta and Prang! Mr. Simpson: Thank you. Wapcaplet: Do sit down—my name's Wapcaplet, Adrian Wapcaplet... Mr. Simpson: how'd'y'do. Wapcaplet: Now, Mr. Simpson... Simpson, French, is it? S: No, sir. Ah, now. I understand you want us to advertise your washing powder. S: String. W: String, washing powder, what's the difference. We can sell "anything." S: Good. Well I have this large quantity of string, a hundred and twenty-two thousand miles of it to be exact, which I inherited, and I thought if I advertised it— W: Of course! A national campaign. Useful stuff, string, no trouble there. S: Ah, but there's a snag, you see. Due to bad planning, the hundred and twenty-two thousand miles is in three inch lengths. So it's not very useful. W... that's our selling point! SIMPSON'S INDIVIDUAL.

MOTEL 6: first left
HBO, Free Local Calls

STRINGETTES! S: what? W: The NOW STRING! READY CUT, EASY TO HANDLE. SIMPSON'S INDIVIDUAL EMPEROR. STRINGETTES – JUST THE RIGHT LENGTH!" S: For what? W: "A MILLION HOUSEHOLD USES!" S: Such as? W: Uhmm...Tying up very small parcels, attaching notes to pigeons' legs, uh, destroying household pests. S: Destroying household pests? How? W: Well, if they're bigger than a mouse, you

that relate to the wind's character. In addition, the same sensor measures both the wind speed and direction resulting in a real-time modulation of the timbre along with the compositional structure. The acoustic architecture of twelve loudspeakers freely suspended from the tower structure permits sound to move up and down in the form of a spiral, thus making the tower's form tangible. The tower is the physical stand around which the sound, like an enveloping coat, is blown by the wind.

Project by Andres Bosshard
(www.soundcity.ws). Year of origin: 2006

chromatic Hybrid Style Alternator," makes ten different styles available: 300 characters that in their permutation offer infinite typographical variety. The font style can be influenced with the help of various control elements of the application.

In addition, data from the immediate environment, such as wind speed and temperature, also plays a role in the design of the typeface. The temperature ranges from -10° F, deep-frozen state: serif font, to 100° F: "Fully Round Informal typeface"; "Warm is nice, so Twin is round and soft." [02] The style can be fixed at points between these values; real-time weather information can determine the style for a day. Such a direct reference is not, however, a fleeting reflection, but rather a visualization of the changing environment of a city. Furthermore, the degree of certain properties can be adjusted: between formal (with serifs) and informal (sans serif and rounded), normal (regular), and bizarre (symbolic and highly variable), as well as hard and soft; the "play" function enables users to set their own value levels. In addition, users of the font can look for inspiration in the automatically generated variations of the Twin Cities Design Celebration Logo that are available. Alongside the conventional representation, character variations were created with cadenced discontinuity, reminiscent of hieroglyphs or HTML code, indicating that the typeface can have different meanings: it can be a character, an independent symbol (for example, the copyright symbol), or code.

Visual identity by Erik van Blokland and Just van Rossum, LettError.
Year of origin: 2003

[02] Ibid.

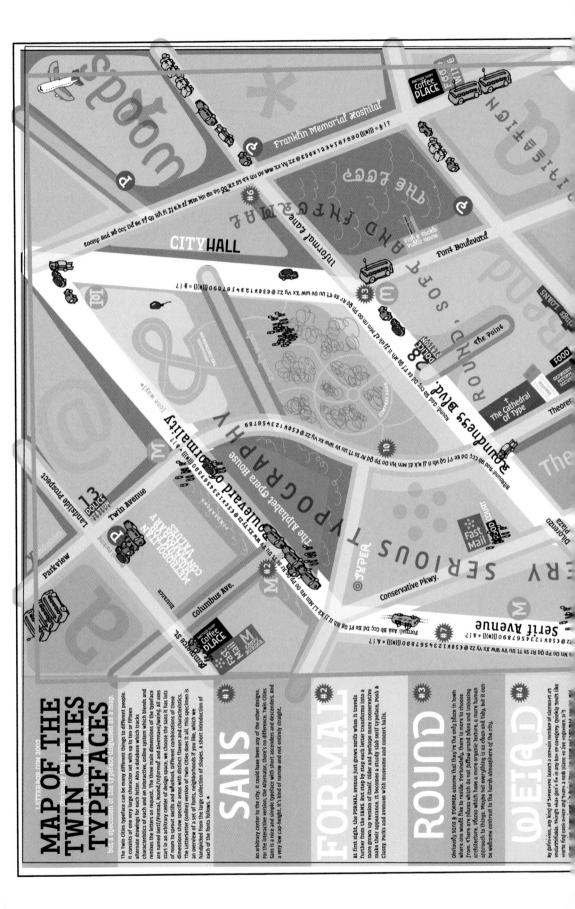

MAP OF THE TWIN CITIES TYPEFACES

The Twin Cities typeface can be many different things to different people. It consists of one very large character set with up to ten or fifteen alternate drawings for each letter. Also a database which tracks characteristics of each and an interactive, online system which blends and remixes the letters on request. The three main dimensions of the typeface are named Serif/Formal, Round/Informal and Sleek+Weird. All axes start in an arbitrary center of design space, we choose the Sans it has lots of room to sprout serifs and whatnot. Different combinations of these dimensions show specific areas with distinct flavors and characteristics. The Lettersetter (online) version of Twin Cities does it all, which we handpicked from the large collection of shapes. A short introduction of each of the fonts follows. ✦

#1 SANS

An arbitrary center to the city. It could have been any of the other designs. For the interactive version, the Alternator, there's no difference. Twin Cities Sans is a nice and simple typeface with short ascenders and descenders. And a very low cap-height. It's kind of narrow and not entirely straight.

#2 FORMAL

At first sight, the FORMAL avenue just grows serifs when it travels further from the SANS. But step by step each letter transforms into a more grown up version of itself. Older and perhaps more conservative make their appearance. It becomes a sturdy slab serif typeface. Push & classy. Parks and avenues with museums and concert halls.

#3 ROUND

Obviously SANS & FORMAL assume that they're the only place in town where one would like to reside. Fortunately, there is more to choose from. There are places which do not follow grand plans and imposing architecture. Places which have a more organic texture, a more human approach to things. Maybe not everything is as clean and tidy, but it can be welcome contrast to the harsh atmosphere of the city.

#4 WEIRD

By definition, any kind of structure leaves a certain number of elements as unclassifiable. Things which don't fit in any box or category. Quickly sorts like... here we find each other and there... a mob place, or the regulars. It's...

The Code of the Tides

"Tied To Tide," a perpetually in motion installation in Sydney Harbour, is triggered directly by the location's natural forces at the same time as it makes them visible. Ten-meter-long ladders that rotate like the sails of a windmill and that are affixed to the ends of suspended beams translate the subtle movement of the wind, convey its strength, and—collectively—sketch its undulations. The beams convey the large movements of the tides. The bow wave of a boat sailing in the harbor triggers a sequence of movements and makes them physically perceptible—not least also because of the familiar harbor sounds: the moaning and creaking of wood and the clinking of metal. A transmission takes place that is also an amplification: observers become aware of natural processes that, taken by themselves, would be barely perceptible.

Project by Jennifer Turpin and Michaelie Crawford. Year of origin: 1999

Figs. 1–2, p. 196: "Tied To Tide"

Poetry on the Road

(Case Study 23)

A Literary Transfer

Commissioned by Adobe, the media artist Ben Rubin developed the project "San Jose Semaphore" for the upper floors of the Almaden Tower, Adobe's new headquarters in San Jose, California. A semaphore is a signaling apparatus whose visual signals can be seen at great distances; with four huge disks lit by LEDs, the San Jose Semaphore transmits an encrypted code by changing position. The illuminated disks rotate rhythmically and stop in a new position every 7.2 seconds. The movement is accompanied by a soundtrack transmitted via an amateur radio transmitter composed of the mechanical ticking of the disks' movement and the voices of so-called number stations: short-wave radio stations that broadcast series of numbers or letters, and at times words. Adobe's Almaden Tower is close to the Mineta San Jose International Airport, and when an airplane flies over the building, the disks react visibly to the disturbance.

Adobe announced a yearlong competition for the decryption of the code, won by two research scientists, Mark Snesrud and Bob Mayo, who

An annual international literary festival in Bremen, Poetry on the Road, "presents the wealth of forms and media of contemporary international poetry and shows poetry in connection with other arts, as visual poetry, experimental sound poetry, in performance and as rap." [03] A form of translation, that of language to visual representation, is made manifest in the visual identity.

The visual identity evokes a translation of the structural level rather than the linguistic content of language. Each year, the poems featured at the festival are visualized with software that is based on another unique principle that generates its own visual motif; authors are represented by an abstract visualization of their poems. In contrast to comparable visual identities, this feature is achieved through computer-based encoding. Differences between authors or their poems are highlighted through the use of a constant principle. The unique motif appears not only on the posters, but also on brochures as well as the cover and chapter title pages of the book accompanying each festival.

The principle employed in 2002 consists of the translation of words into a rectangle, or texts into a dynamic structure. The form and color of each element represents a letter, the angle of inclination the language of the poem. Those who dedicate themselves to cracking the code gain access to all of the poems presented at the festival. [Fig. 1, p. 200] In 2003, the principle employed had as its premise the conception of a whole text as one line, with each letter corresponding to a specified change in the line: a text designing itself. [Fig. 1–3, p. 201] In 2004, words were translated into polygons and poems into polygon clusters, the form of the polygon corresponding to the statistical frequency of the letter in the language. In 2005, each poem was translated unabridged into a tree-like structure, and each word translated into a leaf. The number of letters in a word is reflected in the number of teeth on a leaf, the sequence of letters determines the leaf's shape, and the length of the poem corresponds to its size. The poster represents all the authors' poems as a thick forest. Boris Müller: "I was visually inspired by L-System algorithms. However, it did not make sense to use any recursive algorithms. But I picked up the idea that certain symbols in a text would control the growth of the tree. Specific letter-combinations would create a new branch, others would make it grow stronger. So the final tree-structure would be a direct result of the letter sequence in the text. Therefore, every poem is represented by its own, distinct tree." [04] [Fig. 3, p. 200] In 2006, each letter — following a very old method of encrypting text — was assigned a number. The sum of the numbers of the letters in a word produces the numerical value of the word; for example, "poetry" is represented by the number 99. All of the poems are arranged on a circular orbit: shorter poems are in the center of the poster, longer ones on the outside. The numbers — which can represent more than one word ("'poetry' shares the 99 with words like 'thought' and 'letters'" [05]) — correspond to a red ring, the thickness of which is a function of the number of words with the same numerical value. In addition, fine grey lines connect the words in their original sequence, which makes a repetitive word structure within the poems visible. [Fig. 1, pp. 202–3] For 2007, the principle consisted of translating a word into a picture. The pictures are taken from the Internet community flickr, where they are categorized by tags. "Using the Flickr API, the application sends every word to Flickr and simply takes the first image from the returning list. So if the word 'sun' appears in a poem, VisualPoetry 07 checks flickr for the most popular image tagged with 'sun.' Each word in the poem is replaced by a photo. However, not the entire photo is used. The photo is cropped depending on the length and the frequency of the word. The horizontal axis

deciphered the code with the help of a stationary webcam, a radio receiver, and specially developed image recognition software. The solution: for the entire year the "San Jose Semaphore" transmitted the full text of Thomas Pynchon's novel "The Crying of Lot 49." "Given the artwork's location (the heart of Silicon Valley) and concept (a semaphore), there was really only one logical choice for the text: Thomas Pynchon's The Crying of Lot 49. Although he wrote the book in the mid-1960s, Pynchon's setting is a fictional California city filled with high-tech industrial parks and the kind of engineering sub-culture that we now associate with the Silicon Valley. The book follows the heroine's discovery of latent symbols and codes embedded in this landscape and in the local culture. Is there a message here, she wonders, and what are these symbols trying to tell me? At its heart, 'San Jose Semaphore' is an expression of what Pynchon calls 'an intent to communicate.'" [06] Rubin's work, which deals explicitly with Adobe's business milieu of digital communications technology, is also a critique: "The third principle was to make the code human-readable. Once its

[04] Boris Müller, www.esono.com/boris/projects/poetry05. [05] Boris Müller, www.esono.com/boris/projects/poetry06. [06] Ben Rubin, www.sanjosesemaphore.com/report.pdf.

structure is revealed, the cipher can
be read with the naked eye, recorded
with pencil and paper, and decoded
readily (if somewhat laboriously) by
hand. This human-scale communication is critical to the artwork's concept."
[o7]
Project by Ben Rubin (www.earstudio.com).
Project period: 2003–2006

Figs. 1–2, p. 199: San Jose Semaphore

[o7] Ibid.

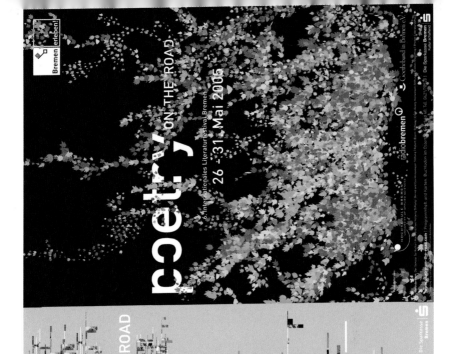

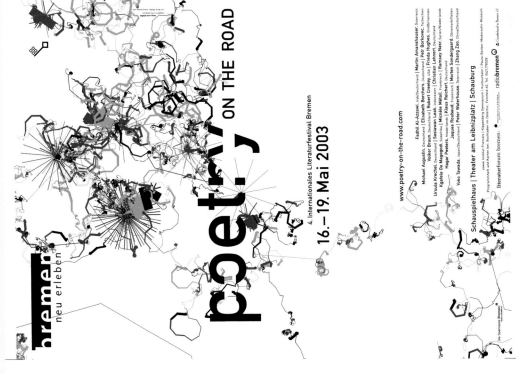

Bremen erleben!

poetry ON THE ROAD

7. INTERNATIONALES LITERATURFESTIVAL BREMEN

11. – 19. MAI 2006

VERANSTALTET VON:

 HOCHSCHULE BREMEN
UNIVERSITY OF APPLIED SCIENCES

radiobremen⊖

⬤ Goethebund in Bremen e.V.

 Die Sparkasse | Bremen |

GEFÖRDERT VON: Bremen Marketing, Senator für Kultur, Karin und Uwe Hollweg Stiftung, Bernd und Eva Hockemeyer Stiftung, Wolfgang-Ritter-Stiftung, DAAD, Waldemar Koch Stiftung, Bremer Literaturstiftung, pro helvetia

WWW.POETRY-ON-THE-ROAD.COM | Programmheft und Karten bei: Buchladen im Ostertor, Fehrfeld 60, Fon: 0421-785 28 | Die Sparkasse

GESTALTUNG: jung und pfeffer : visuelle kommunikation Bremen, Amsterdam | mit Boris Müller, esono.com

is defined by the length of the word, the vertical one by its frequency…. The crop and the position of the pictures are also
determined by the computer program." [o8] In contrast to previous years, this principle corresponds to the semantic level of
the poems. [Fig. 2, p. 200]

Visual identity by Boris Müller (www.esono.com) and Florian Pfeffer, Jung und
Pfeffer (www.jungundpfeffer.de); in collaboration with Friederike Lambers
(poetry o2 [fig. 1, p. 200]), Petra Michel (poetry o3 [figs. 1–3, p. 201], o4, o5 [fig. 3,
p. 200]), and Andrea Schaffors (poetry o6 [fig. 1, pp. 202–3], o7 [fig. 2, p. 200]).
Project period: since 2002

Haus der Wissenschaft
(Case Study 24)

The stated mission of the Haus der Wissenschaft (House of Science) in Bremen is to foster understanding of current issues in science and research among the general public, as well as in schools, in the arts, and in business. "Two universities, three colleges, and a prestigious research institute create a lively scientific environment. These institutions work together in various fields in a spirit of good faith for their mutual benefit. The diverse events of the 'Stadt der Wissenschaft 2005' program generated an even greater readiness for dialogue." [09]

"Events and lectures should inspire people to be enthusiastic about science and learning. Children learn by playing. Adults as well. The visual identity for the Haus der Wissenschaft is therefore a playful system of signs that can spawn an infinite number of variants. It expresses the dynamic character of science, creates curiosity, and conveys the joy of discovery." [10]

Its visual identity is based on four basic figures that can be varied in position, size, number, and color. The specific zero-position is different for each object and set at a defined distance from a common zero-point, while the specific zero-point serves as a reference point for the rotation, position, and size of the elements. The common zero-point is the reference point for the movement of the distinct objects and the movement of the sign family. Each element can (a) diverge from the common zero-point in four steps on eight different axes; (b) rotate completely in increments of 45 degrees, with the exceptional case of elements composed of nine lines in which the individual lines rotate; (c) change its size in ten steps; and (d) assume any color from the color palette. [11] "Which elements occur twice, which elements become 'white,' and what position, size, and rotation angle these elements have is stipulated by parameters from the Internet. The variants of the signs are created by scientific data from the Internet (e. g. temperature or sociological data); size, color, position, etc. of the

[09] Haus der Wissenschaft, www.hausderwissenschaft.de/Das_Haus.shtml.   [10] Florian Pfeffer, unpublished manuscript, n. pag.   [11] Ibid.

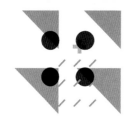

individual elements change as the data changes. From this data
a computer program produces a new sign — that continually
changes but always remains similar to itself." [12]

Visual identity by Florian Pfeffer, Jung und Pfeffer; in collaboration with Boris
Müller (programming). Year of origin: 2005

Haus
der
Wissenschaft

Circus Quantenschaum
30 / 06 / 2005 // 19h

An Oversized Game

"Following up on the original Blinken-lights installation in Berlin, Arcade marks a new step in interactive light installations in public space. In the context of the Nuit Blanche art festival in Paris, the team transformed the Tower T2 of the Bibliothèque nationale de France into a huge computer screen. With a matrix of 20 x 26 windows (resulting in 520 directly addressable pixels) and a size of 3,370 m², the Arcade installation was positioned to be world's biggest computer screen ever... Arcade promoted a new series of classic computer games to run on the screen, allowing everybody to play games on the building. Among others, the all-time favorite pixel puzzle game Tetris could be played using nothing but a mobile phone." [13]

"Arcade" is an installation by Chaos Computer Club e.V. (www.ccc.de). Year of origin: 2002

Figs. 1-2, p. 209: "Arcade"

[13] Chaos Computer Club e.V., www.blinkenlights.net/arcade.

Body Movies

"Body Movies, Relational Architecture 6" is an interactive installation on the main square in Linz. The installation consists of a library of initially invisible façade-sized portraits of residents of Linz. The usual effect of a shadow is reversed as in a panopticon; the portraits only become visible when visitors cover the forms with their shadows. When all of the portrayed figures have been made visible in this way, a new series of portraits is then projected onto the façade, which in turn wait to be made visible by passers-by.

The concept of the work departs from the reality of public squares dominated by monumental sculptures, huge posters, and logos. The shadow projections thus allow the appearance of passers-by to dominate the square in a similar fashion. [14]

"Body Movies" is a project by Rafael Lozano-Hemmer (www.lozano-hemmer.com). Year of origin: 2001

Figs. 1-2, p. 210: "Body Movies, Relational Architecture 6"

[14] www.lozano-hemmer.com/video/bodymovies.html.

Enter! Be Active!

"EnterActive" is an interactive installation in Los Angeles in which an area lit by LEDs incrusted in the ground of a building's entrance area is reflected on the façade. The huge display on the façade represents the number of visitors via illuminated squares and playfully communicates their movements.

Project by Cameron McNall and Damon Seeley from Electroland (http://electroland.net).

Project period: until 2006

Figs. 1-2, p. 211: "EnterActive"

Teleklettergarten

On the occasion of Ars Electronica
2003, the façade of the Kunstuniversität
Linz was transformed into a huge keyboard. "Each visitor can securely scale
the wall. By reaching a red button, they
are connected to an operator on the
ground who guides them from letter to
letter. The climbers go through a kind
of training program and thus for a short
time are converted into software de-
velopers." [15]

Project by Gruppe FOK and Bitnik

(www.bitnik.org/de/teleklettergarten.html)

Project period: until 2003

Fig. 1, p. 212: "Teleklettergarten"

[15] Brigitte Zarzer, Im Zeichen des Codes, www.heise.de/tp/r4/artikel/15/15577/1.html.

Interactive Façades?

"Labeled 'interactive' (which is meant to stand for participation and democracy) the façade is turned, for instance, into a reflective device for any passerby who, willingly or not, controls the appearance of the building, facilitated by some sensor-driven computer software. Some of that 'interactivity' is appealing, but is actually completely arbitrary in most cases. The current temperature, time or some other banal piece of information, reoccurs time after time, and is apparently judged to be important enough to be broadcast at large with considerable technical effort. In other words, the widespread ambition to equip buildings with media surfaces, and the available concepts for content, do not match. It is important to be completely clear about the problem — it is not the financial pressure of some 'evil' industry intending to conquer architectural surfaces to turn them into billboards.

The problem is a lack of cultural or aesthetic concepts that are strong enough to be perceived as beneficial or even necessary for the appearance of the building (and, by extension, cities). We need valid dynamic aesthetic concepts — choreographies — as a continuation of the architectural culture that took centuries to develop!" [16]

"Jan Edler criticizes the fact that the widespread ambition to equip façades with interactive media technology does not match the available concepts for content. It is important to understand this circumstance correctly: '... it is not the financial pressure of some "evil" industry intending to conquer architectural surfaces to turn them into billboards. The problem is a lack of cultural or aesthetic concepts that are strong enough to be perceived as beneficial or even necessary for the appearance of the building.' I completely agree with his criticism. However, the fact that in 1968 the façade

of the Centre Pompidou was already technically equipped to be transformed into a huge screen shows me that the problem has already been in existence for at least half a century. This media façade was not put into operation out of fear that the 1968 movement could take possession of this public megaphone. I understand the continual attempts of art and design to handle architecture with interactive media and to develop the necessary cultural practice 'in public' together. All attempts at the development of such 'technologies' in closed media labs do not make possible any reciprocal cultural learning processes but are only the strategy of an elite that wants to control commercial or political processes." [17]

[16] Jan Edler, Communicative Display Skin for Buildings, in: Branko Kolarevic, Performative Architecture, p. 152.
[17] Andres Bosshard, personal interview, 2008.

Summary

This chapter deals with the creation of interactive processes
from a design and a variable. The variable can be understood as
an impulse triggered by natural forces; and it can also be used
as a control factor that modulates the form of a design. Interaction is coupled with transference, which in the visual identities
described is carried out with the help of a computer. The com-
puter-aided transference uses an algorithm, a finite number of
rules. Rather than a completed, fixed visual identity, the designer
develops algorithms, programs or sub-programs, and interfaces
[18] from which the rules for the visual identity are transferred
and applied in real time. A fundamental distinction is made between programs that control manually developed designs and
those that produce designs and thus purely generative processes.
In the visual identity of the Twin Cities, the design — a typeface
system made up of ten independent typefaces — is developed
beforehand. Although the design elements are fixed, the updated
version of the typeface is nevertheless based on a precisely
composed chain of computer-controlled steps that can be continuously modulated by external control factors such as current
wind and temperature levels to generate the typeface of the day.
Thus a repeatedly re-modulated visual identity incorporates,
constitutively and in real-time, the unpredictable character of the
wind, producing a broadly expressive range. The sound tower in
Stuttgart is based on a similar principle: composed modules,
live-electronic circuitry, and unforeseeable impulses of the wind
interact in a complex manner. The composition extracts of the
sound tower, the typographic system of the Twin Cities, and the
signs of Cité Internationale provide their own characteristic set
of fixed elements that are, respectively, chosen and combined
by external stimuli, combined via a random generator, and char-
acteristically dispersed. The fusion of designed modules and
dynamic code is remarkably useful for imbuing text elements

[18] Eric Olsen sees the font in the visual identity as a service program: "No, I don't think of it as a typeface,
but as a utility." Walker Expanded, http://design.walkerart.org/detail.wac?id=2090&title=Featured%20Project.
Ruedi Baur also speaks of tools in relation to the visual identities of Cité Internationale and Flughafen Köln-Bonn.
Baur, personal interview, 2006.

with significance. The determinate-indeterminate nature of results generates enormous freedom for designers if they have confidence in the unpredictable and if they ally themselves with chance — the results can be richer than ever thought imaginable. Purely generative solutions, as with Poetry on the Road, require the additional recourse of communication design for the semantic layer, as verbal communication cannot be automated. If the visual layer is driven by a physical process with its own conventions, these become visible: in the visual identity of Poetry on the Road, they are aspects of linguistic structure and conventions; in the work "Tied To Tide," they are the wind and the waves, and the sweeping, temporal movements of the tides.

IV.
What Can Flexible Visual Identities Achieve?

Provisional solutions?

"So what is so revolutionary when one assumes the premise that the sign must be variable and is processual … the world is changing: new media. We shrink back from conclusive judgments. No assertions anymore, only fragments, questions, and experiments; nothing aspires to be something 'bigger, more substantial,' we have 'the courage for incompleteness' and everything is in process.… Have we learned something new when our signs are now more liberal and processual, or have we just become more cowardly? Is the flexible sign a good visual identity at all when it wants to negate all traditional qualities of a good visual identity?" [08]

Wide-ranging research into currently accessible case studies reveals that flexible visual identities are, for the most part, commissioned by organizations in the cultural and public sectors. Among the twenty-four case studies, there are twenty visual identities from the cultural sector and four from the private sector. Among them are: eight visual identities for museums [01]; three visual identities for cultural events [02]; two visual identities for public spaces used for cultural events [03]; three visual identities for public spaces [04]; and four visual identities in the field of education, research, and development. [05]
The visual identities from the private business sector are the following: one visual identity from the service sector [06] and two visual identities for companies which produce goods. [07] Case study 3, Ile Seguin-rives de Seine, is a visual identity for a construction site in Paris. It cannot be allocated to any of the groups but can be counted within the sector of private business. Among the examples, it is predominantly visual identities with a cultural reference that are represented. Among the important exceptions are the visual identity of the PTT Posterijen, Telegrafie en Telefonie from Holland, and the Champalimaud Foundation, a private organization that supports research projects in the field of medical science.

What are the reasons for the tendency of flexible visual identities to appear almost exclusively in the cultural and public sectors? If the pure design process — i.e., the variation process — is considered, flexible visual identities could, in principle, also be developed for the private sector. However, the respective variation process significantly determines the type of result, the breadth of the variation spectrum, and the complexity. The type of result

[01] Kunsthaus Graz, Cinémathèque française, Frankfurter Kunstverein, Museum Boijmans van Beuningen Rotterdam, Galerie für zeitgenössische Kunst Leipzig, Museion – Museum für moderne und zeitgenössische Kunst Bozen, Walker Art Center, Haus der Wissenschaft Bremen. [02] 2000 en France (millennium celebrations, France), EXPO 2000 Hannover, Poetry on the Road (international literary festival, Bremen). [03] Ferropolis, Quartier des spectacles. [04] Aktau Marina Residential District Kazakhstan, Rotterdam 2001 Culture Capital of Europe, Twin Cities. [05] Beaux-arts de Paris, SSH Utrecht, Cité Internationale Universitaire de Paris, Lakeside Science & Technology Park. [06] Flughafen Köln-Bonn. [07] ABM Warenhauskette, "Ffm Lounge" (music compilation, Frankfurt). [08] Das Gesicht des Museums, Bogen 4a.

in turn influences its effect and, with regard to certain conventions of perception, also its reception. In relation to their effect
on recipients and the attendant risks, flexible visual identities
clearly differ from static visual identities.

The more a visual identity becomes a complex language and not
"merely" a logo variation, the greater the risk that recipients cannot make the connection between the variations, and the visual
identity dissolves — for them — into its individual parts. Thus,
the risk is greater that the relationship between the visual identity and the organization is imperceptible or not memorable.
One of the main reasons that flexible visual identities appear
predominantly in the cultural and public sectors undoubtedly lies
in the transfer of basic content to the form of the visual identity.
Five of eight museums (Kunsthaus Graz, Frankfurter Kunstverein,
Galerie für zeitgenössische Kunst, Leipzig, Museion – Museum
für moderne und zeitgenössische Kunst, Bozen, and the Walker
Art Center) focus upon collecting and communicating contemporary art. They use contemporary visual elements in their visual
identities that can be read as a reference to the current aesthetics of new media and formats. In the visual identity of the Galerie
für Zeitgenössische Kunst, Leipzig, for example, the aspect of
"contemporary art in Leipzig" is highlighted through the empha-
sis on the location and the date ("here and now"). The linear
structure serves as another element, metaphorically visualizing
the theme of collecting, and can also be read as a reference to
the linear structure of a video image. "A few years later, linear
patterns became the visual identity for the contemporary in general in the Saxony area." [09] This leap gives an indication of the
transference achieved in reception: from elements of the visual
identity to the content of the organization, but also to general
current phenomena and media. Other visual references also produce this relation; for example, the grid-based design in the

Adapt / Transform / Move / Interact

In his investigation "Flexible: Architecture that Responds to Change,"
Robert Kronenburg illustrates four
fundamentally different forms of the
flexible: architecture that is able to
adapt, to transform, to move, and to
interact. "Architecture that is designed
for adaptation recognizes that the
future is not finite, that change is in-
evitable, but that a framework is
an important element in allowing that
change to happen." [10] One of his
case studies is the Serpentine Gallery
in Kensington Gardens, London, UK,
which every year since 2000 has been
offering a leading architect the opportunity to design a temporary pavilion
for the gallery. [11] Shouldn't this unusual idea also be presented through
the visual identity of the gallery, thus
lending it real, significant content?
And would it not be conceivable that,
for example, the visual identity of
a museum could be developed each
year by another agency and another
designer? Coherence would be en-
sured through a superordinate theme
and the respective interpretation
could visualize the motto for the

[09] Markus Dreßen, personal interview, 2006. [10] Robert Kronenburg, Flexible: Architecture that Responds
to Change, p. 115. [11] The following architects have to date participated: Zaha Hadid (2000), Daniel Libeskind
(2001), Toyo Ito and Arup (2002), Oscar Niemeyer (2003), MVRDV (2004) (MVRDV represents the surnames
of the architects Winy Maas, Jacob van Rijs, and Nathalie de Vries), Alvaro Siza and Eduardo Souto de Moura
(2005), Rem Koolhaas (2006), and Olafur Eliasson and Kjetil Thorsen (2007).

year and set an individual focus. With the example of the Seattle Public Library, Robert Kronenburg illustrates the expansion of the field of activity of public institutions. "Koolhaas feels that libraries as a building type have become increasingly compromised by the multitude of tasks they must now undertake in comparison to their traditional role as a book-based resource. Their need to be information stores that respond to all aspects of media has resulted in bland, open-plan floors that allow the flexibility of shifting demands, but also lead to spaces defined by bookstacks and computer terminals. The approach taken with the Seattle Public Library was to create a series of spatial compartments, each dedicated to a specific role." [12] What conclusions can be drawn from this for a visual identity? Just as the Seattle Public Library has extended its field of activity and organized its interior architecture for the purpose, shouldn't it also change its logo — currently featuring an open book and a globe — which lags far behind the extraordinary qualities of the library? It is much too general and unspecific. The expansion of functions also

EXPO Hannover visual identity, in which the pixel-like is expressed, or the typographic spelling reminiscent of HTML code in the Twin Cities and Cité Internationale visual identities. The signs can be read as quotes from our contemporary media and their visual traces. At the same time, a more subtle media variation is carried out: the linear structure is not only an ornament, but translates the structure of an electronic image into a graphic form, thus making it comprehensible. The visual identity is substantially strengthened and gains significance through such references.

But not only are the contents transferred, the basic attitude is also given expression in the visual identity. Museum director Chus Martinez characterizes the Frankfurter Kunstverein as an organization permanently rediscovering itself. The visual identity of the Frankfurter Kunstverein reflects this openness to new ideas and projects in art and art mediation. It does not merely represent this attitude on a symbolic level, but strengthens it in a continually evolving visual identity. By integrating current social and political themes, cultural organizations have the potential to cultivate actuality in the visual identity. Static visual identities accomplish this primarily only on the image plane, as the logo remains constant until a redesign is carried out. In contrast, when stabilizing elements create a continuous direct connection with the organization, flexible visual identities have various design tools at their disposal.

Static visual identities represent a company or organization on a general level, in their totality. "Corporate Design shapes ... the visual unity of form of production, advertising, packaging, company architecture, sales outlets, means of transport, etc.... Brands are the foundation of corporate design. They make iden-

tity recognizable inwards and outwards in that they imprint themselves on people's minds." [13] Specific contents are conveyed
separately through typographic means, a particular layout, and
above all through the image level. The singular logo, the "core
statement of companies and institutions," [14] is characterized
by stability. The effect of stability, continuity, and uniformity is
to make the company or organization always recognizable. With
flexible visual identities, the constant elements assume this function. The variable elements represent changing contents: the
particular as opposed to the general (e. g. Galerie für zeitgenössische Kunst, Leipzig), temporary events as opposed to permanent programs (e. g. Museum Boijmans van Beuningen Rotterdam
and SSH Utrecht), subsections of an organization as opposed to
the entire entity (e. g. Frankfurter Kunstverein, Walker Art Center, Cité Internationale Universitaire de Paris, and Quartier des
spectacles), and the individual as opposed to the superordinate
(e. g. 2000 en France).
In both the business and culture sectors, the specific conditions
reflected in the visual identity often change in very short time
periods, such as when companies merge or their product range
expands. As a result, there is a need for the visual identity to be
forward-looking in anticipation of new contents. With the visual
identity for the plastic profile manufacturer Thyssen Polymer/
Inoutic, [15] a new name was developed and the existing visual
identity reworked. In order to also be able to represent prospec-
tive new content with the visual identity, a name was chosen
that covers a very wide purview. "Companies must be present
in new business fields in today's global stampede.... The window
profile producer can later do a lot under the name Inoutic — for
example, go into design and architecture, build houses or, if
plastic no longer exists, work with completely different materials.
'We very consciously set up a wide contentual dimension,' says

applies to other public institutions,
such as contemporary museums.
In order to endure, a visual identity
should use these changing roles as
a foundation.

 [13] Beat Schneider, Design – eine Einführung, p. 215. [14] Josephine Prokop, Museen – Kulturschöpfer und
ihre Markenidentität, p. 115. [15] Visual identity by Martin et Karczinski, www.martinetkarczinski.de.

Peter Martin from Martin et Karczinski." [16] The broader the spectrum of the visual identity created, the more references it allows — even for the future. And yet, at the same time the degree of generality increases and with it the risk that the concrete, specific idiosyncrasies of a company get lost in arbitrariness, with a possible consequence that it will not stand out sufficiently from other companies in the same sector. The risk increases of course when other companies follow a similar strategy.

If the visual identity is based on the interplay of constant and variable elements that influence each other in terms of form and content, this risk can be reduced. The variable aspects are taken up by the design principle and made concrete in specific situations. For example, the visual identity of the Cinémathèque française is based on such an interplay, in which the basic theme of "light" or "projection" is left general, but made concrete and specific in various media and situations.

The visual identity of SSH Utrecht is based upon a passport photo-like portrait representing a member of SSH Utrecht. This portrait appears with changing characters in the overall visual identity. The portraits not only show marginal differences in hairstyle and clothing, but also represent additional exceptional cases related to specific situations. Pictograms referring to the visual identity are used in building signage. The concrete situation is conveyed in a narrative fashion with a special character derived from the "general portraits." For example, the "handicapped WC" is represented by a woman in a wheelchair from the SSH Utrecht visual sign family. For the announcement of a special event such as the opening of a new building — called De Bisschoppen (The bishops) — a character looking like a bishop simultaneously takes over the announcement of the opening party and the reference to the visual identity. His similarity to the other characters ensures recognition of SSH Utrecht and thus the coherence of the visual identity. A visual identity that responds flexibly and distinctly to special events is considerably more time-consuming and expensive than a static visual identity. This expenditure is partly justified by the fact that a changing program, such as special events, can be announced in a more differentiated way, thus considerably increasing the attention drawn by the announcement. As a whole, the visual identity becomes more significant because it is reinforced substantially by specific content, and an organization benefits from greater differentiation because it can appeal to different target groups.

What design possibilities does a flexible visual identity have when it aims to create references to new contents? Modular elements and references set the precondition to form transitions to pre-existing signs or visual identities. This process is illustrated with the visual identity of the Cité Internationale Universitaire de Paris. When the Cité Internationale appears as a community, such as in the credits of promotional programs, the basic logo is used. In addition, the individual residences bear their own specific singular logos and can thus appear visually independent. The elements of the name are arranged left- and right-justified on an axis formed by the word "Cité." Because of the stepped structure, the logos of other residences can be docked in various positions; it is possible to choose between approximately six different arrangements. The opportunity for the integration of existing content is based on laws of convergence through similarity.

A wealth of forms — here by means of typographic modification —creates a wide range of linkage points for further elements. Ornaments, majuscules and minuscules, and letters that appear handwritten are mixed in the typeface. However, color tones, motifs, and materials also represent potential linkage possibilities.

"It is the staging which in each case also formulates specific strategies for attracting and directing attention. It makes sure that the materiality of the representation is, in each case, produced performatively in such a way that the elements appearing draw the attention of viewers at the same time their attention is directed to the act of perception. It is the staging which on the one hand works towards what is appearing, but also the unimposing and commonplace, being eye-catching and appearing transfigured; and on the other hand perceivers noticing the act of perception, how the movements, light, colors, sounds, smells, etc. affect them and transform them. In this sense, staging can also be defined and described as a process aiming towards the re-enchantment of the world — and the transformation of those involved with the act." [17]

Fully developed flexible visual identities can react not only to the changing contents of an organization, but also to its context. A visual identity is context-reflexive when it takes up something from the context in which it functions and reproduces it. Included here are geographical, architectonic, urban, landscape, but also special cultural and social characteristics. They hold great potential for lending significance to the visual identity of an organization, a city, or a city quarter.

Aktau Marina Residential District, Kazakhstan, is an example of a fully developed context-reflexive visual identity. Like many Soviet cities, the Kazakh city of Aktau — Shevchenko in Russian — had nearly lost its special characteristics as a regional city through decades of socialist domination; a plan to reflect the specific context therefore represents a particularly great challenge. Significant idiosyncrasies found in traditional carpet patterns are reinterpreted for the visual identity: contemporary patterns are created which, in contrast to the originals, are dominated by the surface rather than individual ornament, but that nevertheless clearly reference national folk traditions. Because of their braiding, the pattern areas evoke the carpets with which Kazakh yurts are still decorated today. When the patterns appear in parking lots, streets, or sidewalks, the prosaic is transformed into something special. The revaluation is realized by means of staging that references existing elements.

What distinguishes a real from a staged situation? Staging means making something visible and concealing something else, drawing attention and directing energies that can lead to the creation of something new. In Aktau, like in a montage, elements that originally belonged in very different places are superimposed. Thus, inside and outside, the everyday and the distinctive, tradition and present merge. The reserve of patterns and grids forms endlessly combinable material that can be used on different

[17] Erika Fischer-Lichte, Ästhetik des Performativen, p. 230.

scales. The possibility of combining the patterns — which lend themselves to further development — provides the dramaturgical precondition for a convincing staging of the visual identity, characterized by the ability to design the patterns individually for specific settings, such as signage system elements, streets, sidewalks, and promenade seating. Convincing staging contributes to a unique, distinctive visual identity. A simple eye-catching imitation of Kazakh culture would have been a poor staging; instead, by merely evoking the culture, the patterns create a subtle connection. Such allusions invariably call up various connotations or whole connotational fields, by means of which the visual identity is, in terms of content, more broadly based. Through the staging, the visual identity occupies the entire tableau of the district. In contrast, one imagines a singular logo or the municipal coat-of-arms discretely placed on the edge of information panels. The more real conditions or events are integrated into the representation of an organization or a city, the more re-presentation (via the visual identity and marketing) becomes presentation. The organization or one of its parts genuinely emerges: this real presence creates a degree of authenticity and credibility that static visual identities achieve with difficulty. All signs and symbols that go into the staging represent the organization and refer to real processes engendered by it, representing a detail that, although symbolically charged, nevertheless makes reference to something real.

"Bosch, Helvetica. Lufthansa, Helvetica. Bayer, Helvetica. Osram, Helvetica. Hypobank, Helvetica. Condor, Helvetica. BMW, Helvetica. Honda, Helvetica. BASF, Helvetica. AEG, Helvetica. Deutsche Bahn, Helvetica. Miele, Futura — oops! Thanks very much for your inventiveness, dear designers. If that is supposed

to be design, the world needs no designers." [18] The interchange-
ability of visual corporate culture is documented in a study by the
Damm und Lindlar agency. "Conclusion: appalling monotony....
'A great many visual identities are neither unique nor delimitative,
and neither describe content nor are self-explanatory,' explain
Ulrike Damm and Dorothee Lindlar." [19]

According to Ulrike Damm, one of the causes lies "on the business side when values are set: the firms relate too strongly to
a possible vision. They should focus more on the now and do a
thorough investigation into their particular qualities — only in
this way do distinct values manifest themselves. It is important
to work towards a vision, but it cannot be the core of the identity.
The lack of differentiation continues with the visualization of
these values." [20]

The "now"— the specific cultural or geographical context, the
specific architecture or characteristics of the urban and regional
environment depicted in the example of Aktau — is above all the
activities, processes of change, and even the events of the organization. When visions are formulated with genuinely significant
content of the company or organization rather than attributes,
general values, or cliché ideas, a differentiated visual identity
emerges. Static visual identities have less potential to reference
changing contexts because they run the risk of losing the coherency of the visual identity; the prevailing singular logo cannot
but be retained and thus remain identical. The latitude for variation depends primarily upon how greatly the resources apart
from the logo — typography, colors, visual language, layout —
are fixed. With flexible visual identities, coherence is maintained
as the constant aspects provide stability and only the variable
aspects generate dynamics. In the visual identity of the city of
Aktau, the stabilizing factor is produced with the contentual reference to the richness of Kazakh culture. The dynamic factor

[18] Deneke von Weltzien, Keine Zähne im Mund, aber "La Paloma" pfeifen pfeifen, in: Kompendium Corporate Identity und Corporate Design, p. 152. [19] Ulrike Damm, Über Ursachen und Konsequenzen der mangelnden Differenzierung in der visuellen Unternehmenskommunikation. [20] Ibid.

consists of developing this richness, i.e., its contemporary interpretation, and particular situation-specific application.

Still another reason for an absence of values can be found in the
meaninglessness exhibited by some logos. "If one asks renowned
designers and brand experts, a good trademark, formally and
aesthetically speaking, must be…concise and thus memorable.…
This describes a prevalent design attitude that for the most part
sees its task as developing signs as timeless and association-
neutral monuments. The special quality of such signs lies in their
contentual indeterminedness—they become learnable symbols."
[21] The desired absence of content aims to create a "universal
projection surface" which liberates the company or organization,
making them flexible and leaving them perpetually open to any
type of representation. This approach serves to put the company
into the most ideal market position at any given time.

"Individual values" can only be procured when significant contents are translated into a visual form. An example of such a translation can be seen in the typogram developed by Otl Aicher for
ERCO Leuchten GmbH. "The requirement was to transform light
into typography and to do so in substance and not symbolically.
Aicher regarded the cult of symbols critically; after all, under
Hitler's dictatorship he had experienced the mass delusion and
the symbolic power of the swastika.… A symbolic solution would
have been the search for a type of light source, such as lamps,
bulbs, stars, light beams, or suns as a number of lighting companies use for their 'image building.'… Light, a physical quantity,
loses intensity relative to its distance. Aicher transferred this principle to the typogram, which reflects the shade-giving character
of light." [22]

Does the "cult of symbols" still need to be rejected on principle?
What do dynamic visual identities have to offer in reply to author-
itarian, territorial claims to power? How can visual identities be

      [21] "Their strength is their universal effect in different media. Vice versa their weakness lies exactly in this
          ambiguous breadth of interpretation and association, which however can be met with an appropriate com-
          munication pressure." Matthias Beyrow, Logo und Marke, in: Corporate Identity und Corporate Design, p. 58.
          [22] "The progression begins with the letter E in Univers 65 and continues with the R in Univers 55, the C
          in Univers 45 and ends with the drawn O modelled on Univers." Nadine Schreiner, Vom Erscheinungsbild zum
          Corporate Design, p. 118.

formed without falling back on the canon of symbolic signs?
Aicher's typogram is a rather good illustration of how a basic
theme — light — is substantively conveyed in a graphic sign, i.e.,
through the translation of its mode of action. An accomplished
and coherent translation — into another form of expression,
another medium, between various media — is an important criterion of fully developed flexible visual identities. Signs that represent the organization on a purely symbolic level are often used
in static visual identities. For the Deutsche Filmmuseum, Frankfurt am Main [23] a sign from cinematic history is used — the
observation slits of a "zoetrope," a forerunner to today's film projectors, are arranged in a circle. In the logo of the visual identity
of the Filmmuseum Potsdam, [24] the area around a woman's
eye forms a "pars pro toto" and cites Sergei Eisenstein's "Battle-
ship Potemkin," the eyes belonging to the mother in the famous
scene on the steps of Odessa.

Symbolic signs oriented towards general significations run the
risk of rapidly appearing non-specific and replaceable. In order
to represent an organization effectively over an extended period
of time, they must constantly be "made tangible" anew, i.e.,
realized or made concrete. Fully developed flexible visual identities are not limited to a purely symbolic level; they convey something real, they are performative, which will be described later
in greater detail. "Projected light" is at first considerably more
general as a sign for the Cinémathèque française than the two
examples described above, and thus less significant. However,
substantial physical presence is lent to the sign through the translation of the theme of "light." It is persuasive and believable because it gets to the root of the matter in an intriguing manner, and
is constantly realized anew in specific situations and media.

"Real values" can be most notably represented when an organization's ongoing activities are integrated into the visual identity.

[23] Design by Günter Illner and Phillip Teufel, 1984.   [24] Design by grappa/blotto design, 1993.

With the Quartier des spectacles, the crucial step was not merely
the new design giving the individual venues greater public visibility, but giving them collective visual visibility, even "identity,"
without having to relinquish their own individual visual identities
in the process. As with the visual identity of the Cinémathèque
française, "light" provides the signified, not however in the sense
of "projection" but of "illumination." The illuminated spot directly
indicates at each venue whether it is open to the public, and a
collective lighting concept actively links the individual venues
into a network. Information is coordinated through an online calendar and directly "represented" via the light; the more events
there are, the more lights are illuminated. The Quartier des spectacles events in the evening and at night, and the monthly or
annual recurring festivals are simultaneously progressing "rituals"
which define the rhythm of the quarter, create short and long
cycles, and determine the density of the flow of people. They are
bound to the progression of time and various intensities of performances within these time periods. The visual identity — the
"visualization of the identity"—here is understood quite literally;
what is unique is that the whole quarter becomes more visible,
thus increasing its collective appeal, and, in the process, supports
the individual visual identities. The means used are neither
artificial nor freely invented, but come — to a certain extent self-
evidently — directly from the organizations. The Quartier des
spectacles thus fulfills several criteria of a fully developed flexible visual identity.

The concentrated signal effect — achieved principally through
uniform and constantly recurring means — gives static visual
identities a significant advantage over flexible visual identities.
And while the variations of flexible visual identities allow for

greater differentiation, they also cause dissolution of the concentrated visual message. The greater the number of variable elements and thus dynamism within the variation spectrum, the greater is the dissolution. The use of stabilizing means is required to counteract this dissolution, without which a flexible visual identity risks being neither recognizable nor memorable, thus requiring a greater expenditure in time and money to make the visual identity known and familiar. Designers conscious of this have various design means at their disposal to counteract this risk and stabilize the overall effect. In chapter III, general possibilities are mentioned for how constancy and coherence can be created, and in chapters 1 to 6 they are substantiated on the basis of several case studies.

In a commodity-based economy targeting a global market, uniformity and signal effect generate a highly concentrated message and thus provide a counterbalance to the scattering of locations and products across the globe. And yet, a visual identity that directly references a specific location reduces the disadvantage of greater dissolution. Nearly all the visual identities in this investigation evidence a local focus, whether created for the cultural sphere or the service sector (such as the Flughafen Köln-Bonn visual identity). One exception is "Ffm Lounge," a compilation of tracks of Frankfurt-based lounge musicians, artists, and producers emphasizing its local roots, which is not directed toward a global market. But the most significant exception is the visual identity for the ABM Warenhauskette, whose products are distributed domestically in Switzerland rather than worldwide. There was a greater focus on the inside of the discount store rather than on the outside, as it is mainly the company's own-brand products that were sold at the ABM Warenhauskette stores. These days, individual brand products and lines must compete in the increasingly prevalent store-in-store systems of department

stores. When it was created in the 1950s, the visual identity of
ABM Warenhauskette was a symbol of modernity, which generated—though indirectly—a signal effect. "The serial, the repertoire of combinatorics: permutation, combination, and variation
are the elemental canon of design." [25] Together with Eugen
Gomringer's advertising copy reminiscent of concrete poetry,
this canon displayed its closeness to concrete art. Nevertheless,
the visual identity was suited to the "model of a discount store,"
[26] and was accepted by a broad public as the visual identity
of "their ABM."

In static visual identities, the concentrated, signal-like effect is
mainly achieved through significant reduction. Disproportion-
ate reduction, uniformity, and signal character often lead to an
artificially simplified, schematized visual identity. This is a great
risk because visual identities that appear unrelated and arbitrary
are, given the current overpowering presence of logos, a dead
end. [27] The more significant a visual identity, the more directly
it succeeds in the acquisition of precise visual codes; if there
is no relation between the content and the company, the visual
identity can only be recognized with difficulty. Flexible visual
identities "disproportionately reduce" when one compares the
organization to its representation via the basic logo. And yet this
reduction is counterbalanced by variations in expressive form,
dimension, format, or mediality. The relation between the basic
logo and the variations is a dynamic and complementary potential that represents an important foundation of flexibility.

According to Norbert Bolz, reduction is also necessary in complex
contexts because a uniform visual identity can only be produced
in this way. "Not only the economy but every market segment,
even every larger company is so complex that no perspective or
overview exists anymore. And the following applies to all com-

[25] Urs Fanger, in: ABM, p. 141. [26] Ibid., p. 6. [27] "We are 'confronted with over 2,000 logos every
day'; even the smallest businesses take the view that they can no longer do without a logo." BüroX, Markenästhetik & Logo/Typografie in: Alex Buck et al., Markenästhetik 1999, pp. 31–43. Cited in Josephine Prokop,
Museen – Kulturschöpfer und ihre Markenidentität, p. 117.

plex systems in our postmodern world: with progressive differentiation one must invariably and 'awfully' simplify in order to
still symbolize unity at all. From this we can learn that identities
are always constructions." [28] Does this construction of identity not make communication unbelievable for an organization
from the outset? The uniform logo only marks a border behind
which there can be no unambiguous identity because the people
responsible and the structural conditions permanently change.
It makes absolutely no sense to symbolize unity when this unity
no longer exists. The identity represented through the symbol
is an ideal according to hierarchical systems, but in reality networks and complex dynamic structures are at work. [29] "I think
that we shouldn't limit ourselves to always choosing the one-way
street of reduction from complexity. Other ways are to be found
and invented. For example, it is shown in corporate identity
problems today that all models have failed which prematurely
reduce complexity. The failure of Modernism and the Enlighten-
ment is based on their premature reduction to, for example, an
identity that is closed and given within and in itself. In the future,
it will be a question of how we can deal, aesthetically and ethi-
cally, with more subtle forms of differentiation." [30] Should an
organization that recognizes its dynamic complexity and its networking as a positive value not want to communicate a completely
different visual identity? Is holding on to a static visual identity
not a missed chance and does it not hinder necessary effective
communication? "This lie should no longer be permanently
present in the public sector. For me it is the only possibility for
still believing in democracy at all." [31]

Large organizations are nowadays often structured in groups and
sub-organizations. Whereas in the visual identities of the Frankfurter Kunstverein and the Walker Art Center every area has its

[28] Norbert Bolz in: Kompendium Corporate Identity und Corporate Design, p. 173. [29] "As a departure
from formerly dominant models, temporary, decentralized, and modular forms of cooperation such as project
teams, networks, and strategic alliances are becoming more important. They aim to make the 'steel shell'
(Max Weber) of classical forms of organization more permeable and break it.... Both for individual as well as
for collective bodies there can thus be diagnosed a stealthy farewell to the idea of a hierarchically structured
and centrally controlled organism." Thomas Lemke, Flexibilität, in: Glossar der Gegenwart, p. 84. [30] André
Vladimir Heiz, in conversation with Margarete v. Lupin [31] Ruedi Baur, personal interview, 2006.

own sub-visual identity allocated to it, the visual identities of
Cité Internationale and of Quartier de spectacles have both a
common basic logo as well as individual singular logos. When
more than one venue makes an appearance, the common basic
logo can be seen. The interplay of basic logo and the individual
singular logos allows the overall association and its parts to be
represented: the whole city quarter and the individual venues.
Because in the Quartier they represent very different genres,
their individuality is a very important advertising factor. A singular logo would greatly reduce this individuality through dispro-
portionate reduction. Only a kind of meta-theme could be represented — such as "culture city," "culture island," or "culture
mile" — from which — even with the most innovative design —
a significant visual identity could hardly be developed. Fully developed visual identities create individuality and common ground
through complex sign systems and a wealth of forms and colors:
a kaleidoscope which should reflect the various dreams and
yearnings of visitors.

Flexible visual identities enable greater differentiation within an
organization and in turn partially accept greater dissolution. Its
extent depends upon the stabilizing factors that counteract the
dissolution. Constancy and coherence create stability through
separate elements such as through a logotype or the basic logo,
and/or through the constant aspects of each individual sign in
the sign family or "visual language." The design principle, basic
theme, or rules also create constancy and coherence. If a flexible
visual identity becomes a visual language, the dissolution tends
to increase and thus the signal effect is reduced. In addition, if the
fixed elements, such as logotype or basic logo, move into the
background and are only used for certain applications, such as
when several organizations appear together with their own logos,
the signal effect is further reduced. In this instance, it depends

especially upon whether the basic theme or the design principle is contentually appropriate for the organization. Furthermore, the strength of constancy and coherence depend upon the variability, the range, and the dynamics of the variation spectrum. When the visual identity consists of several fixed elements (e. g., EXPO 2000 Hannover, Lakeside Science & Technology Park, and Kunsthaus Graz), variability is, in principal, limited. Modules and building blocks represent an intermediate stage; here, a number of signs limited from the outset can repeatedly be combined in new ways. The visual identity for Rotterdam 2001, Culture Capital of Europe, is an excellent example of the use of a few basic elements with which relatively high variability is achieved. If the visual identity is based upon open rules, a design principle, or a basic theme, the number of varied signs is already considerably higher or, above all, extendable, and thus very strong dynamics — i. e., differences between the variations — can be achieved (e. g., change of dimension with the Museion - Museum für moderne und zeitgenössische Kunst, Bozen, and change of medium with the Cinémathèque française). This quality makes a flexible visual identity surprising, and enables media-specific implementation that also permits situation-relatedness (e. g., SSH Utrecht) and / or context-relatedness (e. g., Aktau Marina Residential District, Kazakhstan). The dynamics within the variations are relatively large in the visual identity of the city of Aktau: they range from visible pattern to invisible inner structure derived from the pattern, which, for example, determines the lighting on the harbor promenade.

The computer enables the designer to work with a still far greater number of signs (e. g., Cité Internationale Universitaire de Paris, Twin Cities, Poetry on the Road, and Haus der Wissenschaft). The visual identity is very broadly reinforced through the immense number of variable signs. At the same time, the computer takes over the variation for designers, creating the risk that, as a result, their creativity disappears and the presence of the computer determines or even overrides the visual identity. The number of variable signs alone still does not amount to a good flexible visual identity. Rather, it must be supported by a significant basic theme and consistently translated into the variations and specific media. The clarity of a concept is established in an appropriate and compelling relationship between theme and visualization and, additionally, in its recognizability. In the visual identity of the Haus der Wissenschaft, the "position, size and rotation of the elements … (are) specified by parameters from the Internet." [32] Their configuration is also produced with "scientific data from the Internet (e. g., temperature data or sociological data)." [33] However, the relationship between this information and the elements is invisible to visitors of the website, because as every change generates a new constellation, there are no fixed relationships. If it were indeed possible to trace visitor activity, visitors would then become participants in the visual identity, as the concept actually envisages. [34]

What is surprising about the concept of the visual identity for the literary festival Poetry on the Road, is that poems are not illustrated with regard to their content and the symbolism contained within, but rather the structure of the language and the rhythm of the syllables are directly translated into a visual design by means of a generative program.

Tension is generated as the poetry, using a common scientific method, undergoes a quasi-statistical visualization. It may also be said of this concept that it is indecipherable, yet the internal proportions and qualitative features of the composition of the poems are clearly visible. It is evident that only the consistent translation of a clear idea produces a credibly staged choreog-

[32] Florian Pfeffer, unpublished manuscript, n. pag. [33] Ibid. [34] "People should be inspired towards science and learning with events and lectures. Children learn by playing. Adults too. The visual identity for the 'Haus der Wissenschaft' is therefore a playful system of signs which can produce an endless number of variations." Ibid.

Immediacy

Events have something immediate about them, but in every description of an event we are before or after the moment in time. Even when we know that the instant — e. g., an idea or a discovery — is entirely born from the moment, it cannot be directly conveyed either through language or through visual signs. The reason for this hindrance lies in the conditions of speech itself. Speech can always only be mediated. "Neither the subject nor any present can be subsumed in language as such. A (linguistic) sign is always only just re-presentation of something, i. e. it reproduces, also in the chronological sense after the appearance of the object to be represented.… Language as a sign is thus not identical to reality or to what is signified." [36]

With the development of electronic media, increasing "eventfulness" or "performativity" can be observed in many forms of art and culture. [37] In theatrical, musical, and artistic performances, installations, and readings, the presence of actors takes on its own reality. At times the meaning

raphy of signs. Poetry on the Road places literature in a contemporary design context and fulfills several criteria for a fully developed flexible visual identity.

Aren't the loss of clear definitions and the increasing dissolution into different voices, media, and forms of expression also an expression of our time? And, precisely for this reason, shouldn't visual identities be stable and uniform? In this context, does not every flexible visual identity contribute to the separation, breakdown, and dissociation, and encourage the general disconnectedness?

The communication media available to us today enable and demand a specific presence and materiality appropriate to each. If the designers of a visual identity do not deal with the media actively and specifically, their sphere of influence is limited because the specific means of communication used for a particular purpose play a considerable part in the differentiated communication of the content. Content and connecting design principle or basic theme are translated into the various media. In the process, the medium is part of the message.

When the format and content are also designed according to the respective specific characteristics and functions, static visual identities often exclude the logo. As in times when websites could hardly be distinguished from classic print media, advantages arising from the diversity of media and formats are disregarded. Will cross-media visual identities one day be taken for granted as is, for example, the combination of photography, video, sound, and text into hypertext structures? [35]

How information is received depends, among other things, on what medium is used for the communication; for example, the

[35] "A corporate identity program is a set of rules that at best tells something about the coherence of the identity of an organisation. But it also has to define the differ-ences between media like a lightbox and paper or between applications such as a brochure and an annual report. To design a corporate identity partly consists of finding the required balance between coherency and diversity." Büro Petr van Blokland and Claudia Mens, www.petr.net/buro/disciplines/corporate_identity/-/en. [36] Andrea Merger, Becketts Rhetorik des Sprachmissbrauchs, p. 80. [37] See Hans-Thies Lehmann, Postdramatisches Theater, pp. 178–84 and 241–60; and Erika Fischer-Lichte, Für eine Ästhetik des Performativen, in: Kultur – Analysen, ed. Jörg Huber, pp. 21–43.

form of distribution influences the number of recipients but also the value that is given to the individual pieces of information. Each medium has its own specific effect. An example: the constant sign content of Cinémathèque française is light. While the variations are a reflection of the movement of a projector projecting a plane of light, they mainly pertain to the translation into different formats: the change of media; for example, into a graphic representation — where the projection is simulated — or in real, live projection in three dimensions. The major difficulty for viewers is to recognize the connection between the variations and the common basic theme of "projection" or "light" contained within them. It is only through this translation work that they will not only see the "projection" basic logo, but also a sign of the Cinémathèque. This work is considerably more demanding than imprinting a constant logo on one's mind. However, once done, the effect for viewers is all the more enriching because they will be drawn into the world of cinema more immediately and directly. In the foyer, visitors to the Cinémathèque already experience their visit as a transformation of their everyday living space, as an event in a celebratory sense. Because processes can be experienced, visitors are drawn into the situation of which their appearance is a part. The step from the representative appearance to performative effect of the visual identity is thus complete. The performative emphasizes the eventful, processual, transitory, and atmospheric. With visual identities such as that of the Cinémathèque française, the appearance and disappearance of signs can be directly experienced by viewers as a "dance of signs." The aesthetic qualities are intensified by the performative act — the effect of light signs flitting by, the movement of the shadows of leaves from the trees, and the always identical "rain-like" traces on the copies of old films draw visitors into the building. Performativity is linked to the "completion of an act." The visual shifts into the background in comparison to the direct effect of the action; i.e., the re-presentation becomes presentation. Thus, the "familiar distinction between the sign and what is designated, the signifier and the signified ... is undermined." [38]

In relation to the visual identity of the Cinémathèque française, this means that although the sign for "light" still indicates the Cinémathèque, at the same time "light" appears directly as what it represents: namely as light, as projection, shadow play, or eventful sign.

In her essay "Für eine Ästhetik des Performativen," [39] Erika Fischer-Lichte speaks of the palpable strengthening of the performative of all art, which she attributes to the "permanent crossing of the genre borders between the various arts to the point of their complete dissolution." [40] These manifestations of dissolution also characterize our everyday handling of electronic means of communication. We do not only use the computer as an isolated tool, but as a hub for several fields between which a direct exchange of data is possible. With a click of the mouse we switch seamlessly between micro and

[38] Erika Fischer-Lichte, Ästhetik des Performativen, p. 42.   [39] Ibid., p. 21.   [40] Ibid.

IV.   What Can Flexible Visual Identities Achieve?

Presence and eventfulness

macro levels and between various applications and activities. Simultaneously we operate between word processing programs, Internet browser, automatic e-mail updates, web blog, live video, and live chat. We switch back and forth between various projects, communicate with several people on staggered time levels, and copy and paste from one program to another. The superimposition of the levels means a permanent transgression of individual tasks and lines of vision.

Only through digital processing does cross-media design in flexible visual identities really become a matter of course. Nowadays we are in a position to implement a visual identity across media, not only in various formats but also "through and by means of them." In this sense, flexible visual identities are answers to the development of media and a reflection of intrinsic aspects of the zeitgeist. The "dissolution of genre borders" also determines the self-image of the designers of flexible visual identities. They no longer exclusively define themselves in terms of their "classic job description," but are always also image architects and sign choreog-

identity does not only show something, but "acts it out": the projection at the Cinémathèque française, the "flowing around of something" in the visual identity of the Kigali Convention Center, and the "coexistence of signs" in that of the Cité Internationale Universitaire de Paris. In the visual identity of the Quartier des spectacles, it is processes of revealing and concealing: the Quartier actively connects the individual venues into a network through a common illumination concept.

"To understand language as a means of communication only takes in a very narrow area; language is something infinitely multifaceted that we simply reduce to meaning." [41] The projected angel's wing on the WC sign of the Cinémathèque strikes a chord with viewers because — subtle Cocteau quote and surreal allusion at the same time — it flies in the face of the purely functional and transforms the banality of the sign, revealing the poetic in our everyday world. The signs do not recede into their function as designators, but are in themselves something — beyond any sense of designation.

According to Jürgen Krusche, the "aesthetics of the performative" would be situated at these poles: "Appear (vs. fix); perception of the appearing (vs. perception of the appearances); leave undetermined (vs. determine); suddenly appear (vs. availability); show the showing (vs. show something)." [42] Our world is increasingly a world made by people, thus the unexplored is also the world constructed by us. Reflection about this unknown is increasing in literature and art, but also in design. By means of language and images we represent "something"— a theme— and at the same time language and images show how they work, i.e., how the theme is constructed. For example, by breaking through its conventional syntax and appearing in other places, the pictogram in the visual identity of Flughafen Köln-Bonn changes its meaning. On a departure board the "airplane

[41] Marco Baschera, personal interview, 2007.   [42] Jürgen Krusche, Zwischen, Chora und Basho, 2001.

ascending" pictogram indicates the meaning: "departure."
On a large window looking out to the sky, the pictogram is rather
read as an image of an airplane flying away. However, it does not
only change its meaning. At the same moment, the pictogram
indicates its own semiotic nature, it "shows the showing."
"In contrast to the other elements, the representation of people
in Flughafen Köln-Bonn as a silhouette is not simplified. Our
social system that we have built up is boring — everything is regulated and constructed. People must be spoilsports, they must
make this loss of depth and simplification visible." [43] The conventions are confirmed and exposed through the instruments
of the visual identity, i. e., they serve as their own critique. This
is directed against the simplification of signs and sign systems
and against the implicitness with which we serve the conventions
as designers and recipients. The signs of the Flughafen Köln-
Bonn invite visitors to play their own airport game as actors and
thereby somewhat counteract the functionality of the airport.

raphers. The ability to be able to translate one's own approach into other disciplines is indispensable for cooperation in interdisciplinary work groups. In the process, the borders within design become blurred, and beyond them the borders to art, architecture, scenography, and choreography.

In the Flughafen Köln-Bonn, surprising constellations emerge
through small breaks and unexpected changes of position, like
in a joke. Whenever the signs change their positional context —
their syntax — such as the airplane flying away on the window in
front of the sky, when they appear in combination with a silhouette, or even move into relation with a level of reality — as on the
information stand—their meaning also changes. Without relin-
quishing their function, the pictograms have an evocative effect
through their slight opening up; they draw the viewer into the
game by pointing out small mistakes and misunderstandings in
communication.
Constellations suddenly emerging arouse a feeling for the present
because they appear and disappear by surprise. The dissolution

[43] Ruedi Baur, personal interview, 2006.

of familiar sign catenations causes irritation for viewers and their habits of perception. The benefit for the visual identity is that it can attract increased attention with wit and surprise.

So too the visual identity of SSH Utrecht, which fruitfully interrupts the continual repetition of a visual identity that is always the same. In addition to the constant elements of the visual identity, the "bishop portrait" has additional elements that make it into a "bishop," whereby it almost becomes a personalized message. It winks at viewers, putting them in the mood for an opening party of the new building, De Bisschoppen. It draws more attention to the event precisely because it responds to the specific situation, which is far more important for this specific implementation than supporting the stability of the visual identity.

In general, what can be learned from this is that for each specific implementation it must be considered how far it can depart from the basic theme of the visual identity. Should a temporary event or something permanent be advertised? Should the information be conveyed in the direct vicinity of the venue or far away from it? In the Quartier des spectacles, it is particularly the main street, Rue Sainte-Catherine, which invites visitors for a stroll. Among the many impressions thus gained are mixed the various announcements of events on the information columns, which are arranged in a loose chain. The space between them really enables the posters to be repeatedly discovered anew, like one might discover a hidden fountain or a small mask above the entrance to a building in a kind of free-floating attentiveness. If visitors follow the path indicated by the columns on Rue Sainte-Catherine, they will at some point turn off the main street into one of the many side streets and thus leave the "objective level of narration." They will then be accompanied by individual light installations by local and international artists; the content of the information, the material, remains the same, except that the language that weaves it is different — it is more indirect, more kaleidoscopic, and more playful. It has been relieved of its function of conveying unambiguous information and instead awakens the poetic side of visitors and thus atmospherically puts them in the mood for the events. It conveys a festive mood and thus possibly a completely different experience of the evening's performance.

Variation processes are not mere design methods with which variance can be created in one way or another. They determine the type of flexible visual identity to a considerable extent: whether it is based on a logo variation, a sign family, or whether it is a "visual language" — a language-like visual identity. For one part of the visual identities examined, variation is understood as the transformation of a logo-like sign, such as with 2000 en France, C Broadcasting, Expo Hannover, and Kunsthaus Graz (chapters 1 and 2). The singular logo is dissolved into a small number of logo-like variations, which incorporate within them the constants and variables.
The visual identities described in chapters 3 and 4 consist of a constellation of signs, a canon of colors and forms: the sign family. Here the constant manifests itself in a content and/or design principle and thereby removes itself from a concrete element. The variable — different ways of representation or levels of abstraction (Museion, Bozen; Kigali Convention Center), different means of representation (Cinémathèque française, Quartier des spectacles) — then relates to a part of the overall design. When constant and variable are superordinate and no longer an "additional element," the spectrum of variation possibilities is considerably wider; what is more, the visual identity can be changed over a longer period of time. "Could language overcome typography using its own system?" [44] asks Andrew Blauvelt, designer

"Beginning" and "origin"

In "Places Full Of Time," [45] Richard Sennett describes the habit children have of always playing where it is most inappropriate. The elaborately designed play areas especially made for them are avoided and instead children head for empty spaces bordered by only a few isolated trees. "Here, though, is a space where time can begin." [46] With a reference to the literary theorist Edward Said, Sennett distinguishes "beginning" and "origin" within narratives: in contrast to what can be traced back to an origin, which is part of a chain of events with causal links to each other, a beginning arises from a conscious, creative "setting": "this means, in the practical work of making fiction, contriving a scene that does not explain itself, in which necessary information is missing." [47] Following this consideration, Sennett makes the analogy from the narrative to the city and the children: the place they frequent is detached from the function of being a playground and from the purposeful planning of "adults" and their custody. "A beginning is a displacement into present; a place of beginning is where one can

[44] Andrew Blauvelt, Walker Expanded. [45] Richard Sennett, The Conscience of the Eye, p. xiv. [46] Ibid., p. 194. [47] Ibid.

make this displacement happen." [48]
With Sennett one can ask: How …
does a planner (designer) invent
ambiguity and the possibility of surprise? With what means can spaces
— indoor and outdoor spaces —
be designed in such a way that they
enable the creation of discontinuities?
Or does precisely the unexpected
elude any kind of planning? The
answer links up directly to Sennett
and his analysis of Edward Said: the
designer "needs to think in terms of
what visually will make for a narrative
beginning.… A planner hoping to
encourage the narrative use of places
would seek to lift the burden of fixed
zoning from the city as much as
possible, zoning lines between work
and residential districts, or between
industrial and office workplaces.
An architect seeking to create a building possessed on narrative power
would seek one whose forms were
capable of serving many programs.
This means spaces whose construction is simple enough to permit constant alteration; walls of brick are
such weak boundaries, walls of plate
glass are not." [49] Plate glass walls
are highly functional, they are self-
contained, perfect, and have a cold,

of the Walker Art Center visual identity. Language-like visual
identities, such as those of the Cité Internationale Universitaire
de Paris, Walker Art Center, Flughafen Köln-Bonn, and Twin
Cities, generate their great significance because almost every
part of the writing-based communication incorporates the constant of the visual identity within it. The organization then presents itself in every single word and presents itself in the relations
between the words. When the constant of the visual identity
transfers itself to the written level of communication and identity
is conveyed through the written signs, a logo is no longer necessary. Karl Gerstner's pretension, that "the design itself must take
the place of the signet," is then, in several respects, met. When
the overall design replaces the logo, the logo is only necessary
for certain applications, such as in the context of a list of logos.
When the letters, word, or pictogram-like signs become the visual
identity through their design, the sign function is doubled: on
the one hand they represent the organization; and on the other
the respective phoneme or sign content associated with the linguistic sign. The one representational level accompanies almost
innocently the other level so that this is subtly but thoroughly per-
meated by the visual identity. Because the meaning of the words
and signs is in the foreground, direct recognition of the visual
identity is almost impossible. The typographic design must therefore be significant enough so that recipients see a superordinate
connection to the visual identity in it, and it must at the same
time be subtle enough not to disturb the flow of reading. Examples
such as Twin Cities and Cité Internationale are among these
visual identities.
In language-like flexible visual identities, new combinations of
elements repeatedly occur on the basis of a "grammar." These
are less representatives and more like actors: they demonstrate
something, do communication work, are a guidance system, or

a lively staging; whereby in the process they always also create
identity. As actors they embody the constant of the visual identity, a kind of center of gravity, like a character that is expressed
in each of these specific tasks. As actors they contain within them
potential references for future combinations and activities.
They form the basis for dynamic visual identities that incorporate variability, processuality, performativity, non-linearity, and
open forms.

repellent character. No dialogue can
be started on them — whether with
posters, placards, or graffiti. In
the field of the visual sign, to develop
"various programs" means opening
out purely functional references and,
in addition, unequivocal representations including ambivalent ones.

V.
Bibliography
List of Illustrations

Online resources were all accessed between
2006 and 2008.

Abdullah, Rayan, and Roger Hübner. Corporate
Design (CD): Akquisition, Sensibilisierung, Prozess,
Vertrags-gestaltung. Mainz, 2002.
Adlich, Stefan. Personal Interview by the Author.
2008.
Amanshauser, Hildegund. Enjoyable Situations:
Performative Projects in Public Space. In:
Public Art Lower Austria, vol. 7. Ed. Katharina Blaas-
Pratscher, pp. 16–31. Vienna and New York, 2004.
Also available at the author's personal website:
www.amanshauser.net/downloads/
AmanshauserVergn-374glicheSituationen2003.pdf.

Baschera, Marco. Personal Interview by the
Author. 2007.
Bauer-Wabnegg, Walter. Die Marke als Medium:
Vom digitalen zum virtuellen Unternehmen. In:
Kompendium Corporate Identity und Corporate
Design. Ed. Norbert W. Daldrop. Stuttgart, 1997.
Baur, Ruedi. Ruedi Baur ..., intégral..., and part-
ners. Baden: Lars Müller Publishers, 2001.
Baur, Ruedi. Personal Interview by the Author.
2006
Baur, Ruedi. Das Gesicht des Museums, Bogen
4a, Fachklasse Corporate Design. Publication for
a Professional Seminar in Corporate Design at
the Hochschule für Grafik und Buchkunst. Leipzig,
1996.

Beyrow, Matthias. Corporate Identity und Cor-
porate Design, Neues Kompendium. Ed. Petra
Kiedaisch and Norbert W. Daldrop. Ludwigsburg,
2007.
Blokland, Petr van and Claudia Mens. Buro
Petr van Blokland + Claudia Mens. Studio website.
www.petr.net/buro/disciplines/
corporate_identity/-/en.
Bolz, Norbert. Corporate Difference. In:
Kompendium Corporate Identity und Corporate
Design. Ed. Norbert W. Daldrop. Stuttgart, 1997.
Bosshard, Andres. Personal Interview by the
Author. 2008.
Bröckling, Ulrich et al., eds. Glossar der Gegen-
wart. Frankfurt am Main, 2004.
Büchler, Henning and Ingo Zasada, eds.
Shevchenko/Aktau: The Heritage of an Ideal
Socialist City; Microdistricts and the City Centre.
Institute for Urban and Regional Planning,
Technical University Berlin.
www.kasachstanprojekt.de/pdfdownload/
microdistricts_and_the_city_centre.pdf.
**Buck, Alex, Christoph Hermann, and Frank G.
Kurzhals, eds.** Büro X: Markenästhetik & Logo/
Typografie. In: Markenästhetik 1999:
Die führenden Corporate Design-Strategien.
Frankfurt am Main, 1999.

Cavelti, Georges, ed. ABM: Erfolgsgeschichte
einer Warenhauskette; Philosophische Strategie
Design 1956–1989. Zurich, 2005.
Chaos Computer Club e.V. Project Blinkenlights.

Arcade, 2002. www.blinkenlights.net/arcade.

Czernin, Franz Josef. Elemente, Sonette. Munich, 2002.

Damm, Ulrike. Über Ursachen und Konsequenzen der mangelnden Differenzierung in der visuellen Unternehmenskommunikation. Page (October 2006).

Das Gesicht des Museums, Bogen 4a, Fachklasse Corporate Design. Publication for a Professional Seminar in Corporate Design at the Hochschule für Grafik und Buchkunst. Leipzig, 1996.

Der Duden, Das Fremdwörterbuch. Mannheim, 1990.

Dreßen, Markus. Personal Interview by the Author. 2006.

Dyck, Regina. Poetry on the Road: International Literature Festival, Bremen. Festival Website. www.poetry-on-the-road.com.

École nationale supérieure des beaux-arts de Paris. Academy Website. www.ensba.fr/ informations/informationsEnglish.htm.

Edler, Jan. Communicative Display Skin for Buildings: BIX at the Kunsthaus Graz. In: Performative Architecture: Beyond Instrumentality. Ed. Branko Kolarevic and Ali M. Malkawi. London, 2005.

Fanger, Urs. In: ABM: Erfolgsgeschichte einer Warenhauskette; Philosophische Strategie Design 1956–1989. Ed. Georges Cavelti. Zurich, 2005.

Frankfurter Kunstverein. Museum Website. www.fkv.de/ frontend_en/ueber_uns.php.

Frieling, Rudolf. Mapping and Text: Editorial. Media Art Net website. www.medienkunstnetz. de/themes/mapping_and_text/editorial/3/.

Fischer-Lichte, Erika. Für eine Ästhetik des Performativen. In: Kultur – Analysen: Interventionen 10. Ed. Jörg Huber, Dirk Baecker, and the Institut für Theorie der Gestaltung und Kunst (ith), Zurich, an der Hochschule für Gestaltung und Kunst Zürich. Vienna and New York, 2001.

Fischer-Lichte, Erika. Ästhetik des Performativen. Frankfurt am Main, 2004.

Flexible@art. Kunst Universität Linz. www.flexibleatart.ufg.ac.at/ main.php?id=abschluss&zufall=5.

Galerie für zeitgenössische Kunst, Leipzig. Museum website. www.gfzk-online.de/en/ index.php?menue=27&pos=8.

Gais, Michael, and Iris Utikal. Unpublished manuscript. n. d.

Gerstner, Karl. Designing Programmes: Instead of Solutions for Problems Programmes for Solutions. Baden: Lars Müller Publishers, 2007.

Gerstner, Karl. Personal Interview by the Author. 2007.

Haus der Wissenschaft. Institution website. www.hausderwissenschaft.de/Das_Haus.shtml.

Heiz, André Vladimir. In conversation with Margarete v. Lupin. www.n-n.ch/upload/files/

C36_DC_Interview_mit_AndreVladimirHeiz_04.doc.
Hess, Judith. Personal Interview by the Author.
2008.
Holz, Hans Heinz, ed. Lohse lesen: Texte von
Richard Paul Lohse (Zürich 1902–1988). Offizin,
2002.
Husserl, Edmund. Analyses Concerning Passive
and Active Synthesis: Lectures on Transcendental
Logic. Trans. Anthony J. Steinbock. Dordrecht,
2001.
Hyland, Angus and Emily King. c/id: Visual
Identity and Branding for the Arts. London, 2006.

International Red Cross and Red Crescent Move-
ment. Wikipedia. http://en.wikipedia.org/wiki/
Red_Cross.

Jakobson, Roman. Marginal Notes on the Prose
of the Poet Pasternak. In: Language in Literature.
Ed. Krystyna Pomorska and Stephen Rudy. Cam-
bridge, MA, 1987.

Klanten, Robert, Michael Mischler, and Boris
Brumnjak, eds. Serialize: Family Faces and Vari-
ety in Graphic Design. Berlin, 2006.
Klar, Michael. Das Ganze ist mehr als die Summe
seiner Teile. In: Kompendium Corporate Identity
und Corporate Design. Ed. Norbert W. Daldrop.
Stuttgart, 1997.
Kluge: Etymologisches Wörterbuch der deutschen
Sprache. Compiled by Elmar Seebold. Berlin and
New York, 1995.

Kronenburg, Robert. Flexible: Architecture That
Responds to Change. London, 2007.
Krusche, Jürgen. Zwischen, Chora und Basho:
Diploma Thesis, 2001. Theorie-Studien zur
Medien-, Kunst- und Designpraxis STH, ZHdK.
Kunsthaus Graz. Bix Façade.
www.kunsthausgraz.steiermark.at/cms/
ziel/4975814/EN/.
Kunsthaus Graz. The Building Overview.
www.kunsthausgraz.steiermark.at/cms/beitrag/
10201227/4938704/.

Lakeside Science & Technology Park GmbH.
Corporate website. www.lakeside-scitec.com/en.
Lauterwasser, Alexander. Wasser Klang Bilder:
die schöpferische Musik des Weltalls. Aarau, 2002.
Lehmann, Hans-Thies. Postdramatisches Theater.
Frankfurt am Main, 1999. (Available in English as
Postdramatic Theatre. London, 2006.)
Lemke, Thomas. Flexibilität. In: Glossar der
Gegenwart. Ed. Ulrich Bröckling et al. Frankfurt
am Main, 2004.
LettError. A Typeface for the Twin Cities. Studio
website. www.letterror.com/portfolio/twin.
Lichtwitz. Unpublished manuscript. n. d.
Loeb, Arthur L. The Architecture of Crystals.
In: Module — Proportion — Symmetry — Rhythm.
Ed. Gyorgy Kepes. New York, 1966.
Lorenz, Martin. Ffm Lounge.
www.designby.twopoints.net/ffmlounge.php.
Lupton, Ellen, and J. Abbott Miller, eds.,
The ABC's of Triangle Square Circle: The Bauhaus

and Design Theory. Princeton, 1991.

Mandelbrot, Benoit. The Fractal Geometry of Nature. San Francisco, 1982.

Merger, Andrea. Becketts Rhetorik des Sprach-missbrauchs. Heidelberg, 1995.

Michel, Sven. Personal Interview by the Author. 2008.

Morrison, Phillip. The Modularity of Knowing. In: Module — Proportion — Symmetry — Rhythm. Ed. Gyorgy Kepes. New York, 1966.

Museion - Museum für moderne und zeitgenös-sische Kunst, Bozen. Museum website. www.museion.it/#das_neue_museion&de.

Museum Boijmans van Beuningen Rotterdam. Museum website. www.boijmans.rotterdam.nl/en/5/many-sided-museum.

Musil, Robert. In: Martin Menges. Abstrakte Welt und Eigenschaftslosigkeit, Eine Interpretation von Robert Musils Roman "Der Mann ohne Eigen-schaften" unter dem Leitbegriff der Abstraktion. Frankfurt am Main, 1980.

Moser, Jeannine, and Franziska Weissgerber. Unpublished manuscript. 2008.

Müller, Boris. Esono.com. Personal website. www.esono.com/boris/projects/poetry05.

Nachtwey, Jutta. Corporate Design im Wandel. Page (May 2006).

Pfeffer, Florian. Unpublished manuscript. n. d.

Place, Jean Michel, ed. Köln Bonn Airport: Cor-porate Design / Intégral Ruedi Baur et associés.

Paris, 2003.

Portoghesi, Paolo. Nature and Architecture. Milan, 2000.

Prokop, Josephine. Museen - Kulturschöpfer und ihre Markenidentität: Eine Untersuchung der Erscheinungsbilder von Museen und Ausstellungs-institutionen in Deutschland, der Schweiz und Österreich. Dissertation submitted to the Univer-sität Wuppertal, Department of Architecture, Design, and Art, 2003. http://elpub.bib. uni-wuppertal.de/edocs/dokumente/fb05/diss2003/prokop/index.html;internal&action=buildframes.action.

Realities:united. Studio website. www.realities-united.de.

Reineck, Antje. Unpublished manuscript. n. d.

Rotterdam 2001 Culturele Hoofdstad van Europa, Programma 2001. Amsterdam, 2000.

Rubin, Ben. San Jose Semaphore. www.sanjosesemaphore.com.

Sauerwald, Martina. John Cage: Fontana Mix (1958). www.straebel.de/praxis/text/t-cage-fontana.htm.

Schedler, Clemens Theobert. Unpublished manuscript. n. d.

Schmittel, Wolfgang. Process Visual: Develop-ment of a Corporate Identity. Zurich, 1978.

Schneider, Beat. Design - eine Einführung; Ent-wurf im sozialen, kulturellen und wirtschaftlichen Kontext. Basel, 2005.

Schreiner, Nadine. Vom Erscheinungsbild zum
Corporate Design: Beiträge zum Entwicklungs-
prozess von Otl Aicher. Dissertation thesis submitted to Bergische Universität Wuppertal,
Department of Architecture, Design, and Art,
2005. http://elpub.bib.uni-wuppertal.de/edocs/
dokumente/fbf/kommunikationsdesign/
diss2005/schreiner/df0501.pdf.

Schwenk, Theodor. Sensitive Chaos:
The Creation of Flow-ing Forms in Water and Air.
Trans. J. Collins. Sussex, 1996.

Sennett, Richard. The Conscience of the Eye:
The Design and Social Life of Cities. New York,
1990.

Sennett, Richard. The Corrosion of Character:
The Personal Consequences of Work in the New
Capitalism. New York, 1998.

Walker Expanded. Andrew Blauvelt in conversation with Eric Olson, Chad Kloepfer, and Emmet
Byrne. June 2005. Walter Art Center. http://
design.walkerart.org/detail.wac?id=2090&title=
Featured%20Project.

Welsh, Alfred Hix. Studies in English Grammar:
A Comprehensive Course for Grammar Schools,
High Schools and Academies (1899). Ed. James M.
Greenwood. New York, 2009.

Weltzien, Deneke von. Keine Zähne im Mund,
aber "La Paloma" pfeifen. In: Kompendium Corporate Identity und Corporate Design. Ed. Norbert
W. Daldrop. Stuttgart, 1997.

Wittgenstein, Ludwig. Philosophical Investigations (1953). Trans. G. E. M. Anscombe. Sussex,
1991.

Zarzer, Brigitte. Im Zeichen des Codes. Presented
at Ars Electronica 2003. September 6–11, 2003,
Linz, Austria. www.heise.de/tp/r4/artikel/15/
15577/1.html.

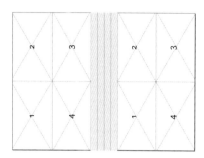

The horizontal illustrations are numbered clockwise starting from the bottom left.

Agricultural Research Center, U.S. Department of Agriculture, http://upload.wikimedia.org/wikipedia/commons/a/a7/Snow_crystals_2b.png

Fig. 1, p. 128: Parts of a Meccano construction kit, www.schraube-und-mutter.de/parts/teileliste_1960/teileliste_1960.html

Fig. 1-2, p. 130; fig. 1-3, p. 133: Intégral Ruedi Baur et associés (reference material, project presentation)

Figs. 1-2, p. 131, figs. 1-4, p. 132: Intégral Ruedi Baur et associés, Aktau Marina Residential District, Kazakhstan

Figs. 1-3, p. 134: Studio Dumbar, Champalimaud Foundation; photography: Dieter Schütte

Fig. 1, p. 136: Markus Dreßen and Kerstin Riedel, with Günter-Karl Bose (project direction), "The Nose" poster (opera by Dmitri Shostakovich) from the poster series for Oper Leipzig

Fig. 1, p. 137: Karl Gerstner, Teddymat, Teddy 75, and Roby 75

Figs. 1-2, p. 138; fig. 1, pp. 140-41: Ernst and Ursula Hiestand, ABM Warenhaus

Figs. 1-3, p. 142; figs. 1-3, p. 145; fig. 1, pp. 146-47: Armand Mevis and Linda van Deursen, Rotterdam 2001, Cultural Capital of Europe

Figs. 1-3, p. 148; figs. 1-4, p. 151; fig. 1, pp. 152-53: Studio Dumbar, SSH Utrecht

Fig. 1, p. 150: Redrawn from Yumi Takahashi and Ikuyo Shibukawa, Color Coordination (Tokyo, 1985), pp. 114-15. In: Edward R. Tufte, Envisioning information. Cheshire, CT, 2005, p. 33.

Figs. 1-6, p. 154; figs. 1-2, p. 155: Schweizerische Fachstelle für Alkohol- und andere Drogenprobleme and Atelier Grand, Sierre, "Alkoholprobleme gehen uns alle an – reden wir darüber" poster series.

Fig. 1, p. 158: Leopoldo

Figs. 1-4, p. 161; figs. 1-4, p. 162; fig. 1, pp. 164-65: Intégral Ruedi Baur et associés, Cité Internationale Universitaire de Paris

Figs. 1-4, p. 167; fig. 1, pp. 170-71; figs. 1-2, p. 172: Andrew Blauvelt and Chad Kloepfer, Walker Art Center; in collaboration with Eric Olson (font programming), Scott Ponik (design of Walker self-mailing envelope) [see fig. 4, p. 167], Walker Design Department (design of Walker Calendar) [see fig. 1-2, p. 172]. Fig. 2, p. 167: photography: Chad Kloepfer; figs. 1 and 3, p. 167; Fig. 2, p. 172: photography: Cameron Wittig

Fig. 1, p. 173: Gyorgy Kepes, ed., Module — Proportion — Symmetry — Rhythm, p. 2.

Figs. 1-4, p. 175; figs. 1-3, p. 176; figs. 1-2, p. 186: Intégral Ruedi Baur et associés, Köln-Bonn Airport.

Fig. 1, p. 178: Mauricio Kagel, Transición II for piano, percussion and two tape recorders. In: Boguslaw Schäffer: wstep do kompozycji, introduction to composition. Warsaw, 1976, p. 399.

Fig. 2, p. 178: John Cage, Fontana Mix, www.medienkunstnetz.de/works/fontana-mix

Fig. 1, p. 179: arndalarm, Zollverein School in Essen, www.flickr.com/photos/arndalarm/338596401/sizes/o/in/photostream

"Design in context"
Volume 1
Dynamic Identities in Cultural
and Public Contexts

Publishers: Lars Müller Publishers
Author: Ulrike Felsing, Design2context
Design concept and layout:
Ilka Flora, Ulrike Felsing
Translation: Steve Gander
Copyediting: Jonathan Fox
Picture editing: Jürgen Hankeln
Production: Marion Plassmann
Printing: FGB Freiburger Graphische Betriebe,
Freiburg

Lars Müller Publishers
5400 Baden/Switzerland
www.lars-mueller-publishers.com

Printed in Germany

ISBN: 978-3-03778-163-0 (English)
ISBN: 978-3-03778-162-3 (German)

Acknowledgements
We would firstly like to thank the designers and
artists who have made this investigation and pub-
lication possible with their kind permission to use
their works and pictures.
Printed with the financial support of the Design
Department of the Zürcher Hochschule der Künste,
ZHdK, with the approval of Jacqueline Otten,
Director of the Design Department.

Also in our programm:

Des/Orientierung 1, Design2context
978-3-03778-133-3, German, English, French

Des/Orientierung 2, Design2context
978-3-03778-158-6, German, English, French

The world's fairest city, Features of Urban Living
Quality, Design2context 978-3-03778-186-9

Ruedi Baur, Intégral, Anticipating, Questioning,
Inscribing Distinguinshing, Irritating, Orienting,
Translating. 978-3-03778-134-0

Design2context
Institute for Design Research
Zurich University of the Arts
Department of Design

Hafnerstr. 39, P.O. Box
CH-8031 Zürich 5
T +41 43 44 66 202
F +41 43 446 45 39
www.design2context.ch
www.zhdk.ch